Brotha Poet Speaks
"Blossom Where You Are Planted"

VONTEZ

Destiny's Publications
P.O. Box 58726
Cincinnati, Ohio 45258

This book is a work of fiction. Names, characters, places, and incidents are products of the author's imagination, or are used fictitiously. Any resemblance to actual events or locales or persons, living or dead, is entirely coincidental.

©2023 by Ronald Vontez Williams

All rights reserved. No part of this book may be reproduced in any form or by any means whatsoever. For information write Destiny's Publications.

Cover design: Consandra Wright
Editor: Regal Rhythms Poetry LLC

Manufactured in the United States of America
ISBN: 979-8-9878729-0-1

Table of Contents

Dedication 7
Special Acknowledgements 7
Introduction Poem 8
100 Movie Titles- The Love Poem 9
100 T.V. Shows – The Love Poem 12
Drop a Jewel On Em' 15
100 Song Titles- The Love Poem 18
A Birthday Poem for Ronesha 21
A Birthday Poem for Nyshayla 22
Happy Birthday Mama 23
How Do I Say Goodbye 24
    Tribute to Reggie Spiller, "Big Reg" 24
Can I Get That Chance 26
An Ohio DRC Experience 29
Don't Worry 31
Missing You 33
The Question 34
Happy April Fool's Day 35
My Responsibilities as a Man 37
Revolving Door 38
How Can I Trust You 41
Polish Up 43
The Spirit of Discontent 45
Jesus Paid the Price 46
What Happened? 47
Testimony: Part 1 48

Testimony : Part 2	49
When I Fell in Love With You	51
What is My Purpose?	53
I'm Back	54
Waiting for my 1st Visit	56
New-Age Slavery	58
Rest in Peace Sistah Maya	60
Mothers, Daughters, and Sistahs	61
Nervous	63
Fight the Power	64
Ossie and Ruby Dee	66
Fed up	67
Looking for Love in All the Wrong Places	68
The Company You Keep	69
My Legacy	71
Are You Who I've Prayed For	73
Let Me In	74
Love	75
Thank God for My Problems	77
I Know I've Been Changed	78
I'm Ashamed of Some of Our Black Men	79
Epiphany	81
Proud of You	83
The Maze of Your Existence	84
Board Game of Love	86
Why Are You So Mad at Me?	87
Life's Doors	89
The N-Word	91
The Continuation of the Dream	92

Domestic Violence	94
Life Lessons	96
Full-Potential	98
Still Waters	100
"My Commentary"	101
Pleasure to Meet You	103
When Will It End	105
Happy Graduation	107
We've Come a Long Way	108
Journey of My Smile	109
Not Forgotten	111
For My Cousin Jimmell	111
Promises Unfulfilled	112
Anointed Message	113
Scandal of Your Love	115
A Love Poem	116
Child Abuse	117
Holiday Blues	119
Being In-Love	120
The Way I Play the Game	121
Do Black Lives Matter?	123
A Bengals Poem – Who Dey	125
Engage the World	127
New Year Resolutions	128
2014 in Review	130
Wait for Me	132
Black History	133
I Love What You Bring to the Table	135
I Wanna Thank You God	137

I Wanna Go Home 139

Respected Man 140

Who Are You 141

Imagine if Women Were Cars 142

It's Time to Wake Up 144

Public Service Announcement 146

Find Out Who You Are 148

Prison Greeting Card 150

Desire 151

Another Prayer 152

Prison Greeting Card Pt.2 153

If I Came with Instructions 154

Give Me My Flowers Now 156

Aging Love 157

Who Got Next? 158

A Glorious Story 160

I Cry for My People 162

The Land of the Free 163

Vocal Defecation 165

Welcome to the Jungle 168

The Revolution Will be Televised 169

Depression 171

You'll Understand Once You Get Older 172

Beauty is More Than Skin Deep 174

Be the King You Were Meant To Be 176

Message to Young Black Men 179

Dedication

This book is dedicated to all the poets in my family! The ones who inspired me to find my voice. My daughter, Ronesha Williams, my brother, Richard Williams... my cousin, Andre Tinsley, and my brother from another, Clay Brayboy. I thank you all from the bottom of my heart for inspiring my lyrical journey.

Extra, special thank you and acknowledgement to my cousin, Leon Terry Jr. for challenging me to write my first poem. I thank you for being the spark of influence that ignited the poetic flame in me.

Special Acknowledgements

I want to give a special acknowledgement to my wife, Dr. Lisa Williams for always being so supportive and encouraging. Also, I would like to thank three special ladies in poetry for inspiring and encouraging me to pursue my passion: Kimberly "DuWaup" Bolden, Symana "She Speaks" Dillingham, and Moneeca "MoPoetry" Phillips.

Introduction Poem

My intestinal fortitude, mixed with a huge mental aptitude,
Is a deadly combo; like a George Foreman one-two,
With a confidence that borders arrogance,
A polished disposition exhuming humbleness,
Where brawn meets brain,
Very handsome, but still 100% masculine,
Totally transparent, there's no masking him,
Well versed but still learning,
A calm demeanor, but the fire's still burning,
A grown-ass man, yet still being refined,
Conjuring wicked thoughts, from a beautiful mind,
Ruled by God, yet was given free will,
Don't bother nobody, but if provoked, I will Kill Bill,
A rose thru the concrete that's still rising,
I've arrived on schedule, but my appearance is still surprising,
Now, you may ask who I be,
Well, I used to go by Ron C,
And for those who don't know it,
Now just call me Brotha Poet.

100 Movie Titles- The Love Poem

"Why did I get married?," probably because your love has me "Gone with the Wind" or is it because you used your "Lethal Weapon" to leave me in a "School Daze," causing a "Butterfly Effect" on my "Life." All I want to do is "Do the Right Thing," like when "Harry Met Sally." So, there's no need to "Rush Hour" into what we have or to be "Fast and Furious" with the "Heat" we share. I want to be one of the "Goodfellas" and love you with "The Passion of the Christ," because I "Die Hard "every time you're "Far and Away." I'm no "Forest Gump," so please don't "Cast Away" my love. Cause "I Can do Bad By Myself," and I'm tired of "Sleeping with the Enemy," and I don't want to be an "Enemy of the State," my "Sleeping Beauty." I want to turn in my "Players Club" card and enter into the "Matrix" with you. We could take a "Journey to the Center of the Earth" or we could "Star Trek." It's your option. I'm so serious… no "Pulp Fiction," or our "Final Destination" could be my "Barber Shop," or a "Friday," or I could drop you off at the "Beauty Shop." Whatever you want in your "Pursuit of Happiness." So, don't make this complicated like "The Chronicles of Narnia," because I wanna be your "Ironman," your "Spiderman," your "Superman," and your "Incredible Hulk." We could start our own "New Jack City." We could have our own "Karate Kid," or a bunch of lil "Bad Boys" my "Precious." Cause, I don't want this to be a one-sided love affair like "Fatal Attraction" while you have me "Waiting to Exhale" or walking a "Green Mile." Because, if I could build a woman like they did in "Weird Science," I would make you my "National Treasure." I come at you with no deception, cause I'm no Decepticon off "Transformers." I'm more like your "G.I. Joe" and I won't treat you like a hoe. Because, if we were "Coming to America," I'd make you my "Queen" even before we'd reach landfall having you screaming, "Are We There Yet." See, this is my "Training Day" in preparation for your "Cinderella Story." I've got my "Anger Management" under control. So, please don't "Blow" this opportunity at a "Sea of Love." Cause, I'll go the "Longest Yard" for you. I have a "Sixth Sense," that we could live in a "City of Angels." And, if you were a "Ghost," well, I would be your "Ghostbuster." No "Poltergeist" or "Exorcist" needed. Cause I'll be your "Demolition Man," your "Rambo," your "Commando," and your "Universal Soldier." No matter how "Rocky" the road gets, I'll be your "Passenger 57," your "Robin Hood" your "Boyz in Da Hood," but not a "Menace to Society." Cause girl, you got the "Juice." Now ain't that "Poetic Justice." Baby, these ain't "Fast Times at Ridgemont High." Nor, are we spending a "Weekend at Bernies." Because after "The Day After Tomorrow," I still want to explore your "Beautiful Mind." I want you to make my "Black Snake Moan." You could leave scratches on my back like "Edward Scissorhands" having a "Nightmare on Elm Street" on

"Halloween" night. So, "Guess Who's Coming to Dinner?" Your "Black Knight," your "Babyboy," your "American Gangster," your Black God Father." So "Scream," but this ain't no "Scary Movie." It's more like a "Toy Story" and your "Black God Father." So "Scream," but this ain't no "Scary Movie." It's more like a "Toy Story" and you're my black "Barbie." I'll be your "Lion King" and your "King Kong." Cause "Babe," you give me "Happy Feet" leaving me "Dancing with Wolves." I want to go "Deep Cover" like Omar Epps in "In Too Deep." I want you to be "My Girl," simply because the "Romeo Must Die" inside of me, and because I don't want to "Never Die Alone."

100 T.V. Shows – The Love Poem

Baby it's "All About You." I'm ready to take the "Quantum Leap" with you, so we can be "Married with Children" and have our own little "Brady Bunch." "As the World Turns" into the "Days of Our Lives," I realize that we're not a rich couple like on "The Cosby Show," but that doesn't matter. Because, we could be as broke as the "Beverly Hillbillies" before the money or live in a "Pettycoat Junction." That wouldn't matter to me. "Sanford and Son" could be our neighbors in "Mister Roger's Neighborhood" with "Big Brother" and "TMZ" shining a "Candid Camera" in our faces like we're "America's Next Top Model," and I wouldn't call the "Cops" or "NYPD Blue." Because, sometimes people have to get "Too Close for Comfort" just to see for themselves if what their seeing is really real. And what we have is a "Real World" "Love and HipHop." So, I don't have to search for the "Flava of Love" anymore, because "Happy Days" are here to stay. "Tamar and Vince" ain't got nothing on us, "Mork and Mindy" would be jealous of what we share. "Mike and Molly" would have to go see "Dr. Phil" and "Dr. Oz" just to understand that I've been "Touched By An Angel" on this "Highway to Heaven." "Moonlighting" is not an option for me anymore. Because, baby you are "Charmed." So, there's no need for me to ring the alarm, cause, I've been "Saved by the Bell" and now we are

"Bosom Buddies" ready to make some "Family Ties." Because to me, "Family Matters" and that's just the "Facts of Life." So "Gimme a Break," because it's "Different Strokes" for different folks and you're making me feel like I'm living in a "Different World." So, I'll go on "People's Court" and face questioning from "Matlock" and "Nancy Grace" to prove my love for you. You can have "Hammer," "Cannon," and "Jake and the Fatman" check my "X-Files," and my "Rockford Files," and they will say this "Fall Guy," this "Family Guy," this "American Dad," well, he loves you for real. So, once we tie the knot there will be no "Divorce Court" for us. So, you can call "Judge Judy," "Judge Joe Brown", and "Judge Mathis" and tell them you're my "A-Team," my "Hogan's Hero," and my "Greatest American Hero." Because "In the Heat of the Night," I don't ever want to be "Living Single" again. You're my homie, lover, and we are "Friends." I just want to hop on "The Love Boat" with you and get "Lost" on "Gilligan's Island." We'll make it our own little "Fantasy Island" and play "Survivor." And I'll make you a "Baywatch" bikini out of coconuts. I'll get my "Magnum P.I." on and we'll be "Dancing with the Stars" brighter than "Friday Night Lights." Baby, you make my "Saturday Night Live," my "Sunday's Best," and my "Monday Night Raw." I see things in you, that in other girls I've never saw. So, there will be no "Tuesday Night Fights" for us. We won't be "Wild N Out" on a Wednesday. And if I were "Scooby-Doo," well, you'd be my "Dog Whisperer." If

I ever found myself without you, I would feel like the "Biggest Loser" and I would have to call "Dr. Drew" to put me on "Celebrity Rehab." Because, I couldn't cope without hearing the word of God from "Joel Osteen" himself, or I would have to fellowship at "The Potter's House" with Pastor T.D. Jakes. But, neither one of us are fake. Our love is as solid as "30 Rock," and your pretty girl swag reminds me of Jenny from the block when she was on "In Living Color." So let me call up Johnny Fever from "WKRP in Cincinnati" or let me email "Dateline NBC," or Alex Trebek from "Jeopardy." Cause, I want to tell the world that I hit the "Wheel of Fortune" when I found you. No "House of Pain" thru the "Growing Pains." We'll move up together like the "Jeffersons" to our own "Pee-wee's Playhouse," or we could move down south to "Dallas," and I'll get "Walker Texas Ranger" to stand guard over our "Falcon Crest." Call me Elliot Ness, but together we're the "Untouchables." Luke and Laura from "General Hospital" could crash and kill "Ally McBeal" and "Tracy Ulman" on the "Carol Burnett Show," and we would laugh like they're in the front row at the Apollo, because baby, my love for you is just that serious.

Drop a Jewel On Em'

My birthstone is diamond,

so every now and then when I speak,

I might drop a jewel.

Using words of love as a weapon of mass restoration,

because that's what believers in Christ should do.

I believe that each one should teach one,

and my Grandma Daisy taught me the "Golden Rule."

That's why I hate to see our young brothas

running around actn' like fools,

but still thinking it's cool.

I so badly want to teach them,

but it's so very hard to reach them.

All they understand is chaos and calamity.

They can't think straight, because they have a warped

perception of reality,

and Kush ain't helpn'

but that's all by design.

The media and the powers that be using the idiot-box to

saturate they minds,

with degraded images of my people,

and if that ain't evil,

I don't know what is,

because some of these kids are having kids,

but can't teach them shit but mindless behavior.

Now let that savor on your mental for a sec,

a child who's been neglected and only teach neglect.
They might try to show love thru gifts,
but believe me young man that isn't it.
You see your presence in your child's life is far more
important than the presents you give out of guilt,
so grab up some stilts,
and step up to the plate, before it's too late,
and you create another you,
who's skillful in his own right,
but haven't been given the proper tools to use.
So, fuse some of that street swag,
along with being a good dad,
and cook that up in your Pyrex pot.
We're doing our children a disservice,
if we don't show them that they are worth it.
With patience, time and understanding,
and if that's too demanding,
well, your priorities are not in the proper order.
Putting money, cars, and clothes before your sons and
daughters.
We place our importance on ignorance,
shiny things of no significance,
when the real stars are right before our eyes.
So, instead of investing money on rims and cars
we need to invest in our youth,
and not just tell them, but show them the truth.

Not just preach to them, but teach them,

because no matter what we say…

Their always looking at the examples that we lay.

Like I said, my birthstone is diamond,

so, every now and then, when I speak I might drop a jewel,

using words of love as a weapon of mass restoration,

because that's what believers in Christ should do.

100 Song Titles- The Love Poem

I'm living "For the Love of You" "My, My, My" "Tenderoni": I feel a "Summer Breeze" whenever you "Walk This Way." So, baby won't you just "Stay" a little while. Cause I love your "Smile" "Wild Thang." "Coming From Where I'm From" I love an "Around the Way Girl," but "You Must be a Special Lady" and a very exciting girl, cause you got me sitting "On Top of the World." You are a "Smooth Criminal" the way you stole my "Achy Breaky Heart" "Brown Sugar." Making me "Float On" like I got "Pretty Wings" and I ain't even drunk no red bull. And baby, this ain't no bull. We're just "Ordinary People" "Climbing a Stairway to Heaven" and I "Never Would Have Made It" without you. "Temptations" are everywhere, but I stay focused on yo "Rumpshaker" while you're "Doing Da Butt." "Make Em' Say Umm" Na Na Na with your fine ass. I'm an "Atomic Dog," but somehow you got me under "Control" with your "Pleasure Principal." So, I won't have to "Call Tyrone" to give me a ride cause "When a Woman's Fed Up" it ain't nothing you can do about it. But baby that ain't got nothing to do with us. Cause I am "Lost Without You." I can't help myself my "Candygirl," my "Tender Love", my "Telephone Love" and I'm your "Mr. Telephone Man." Like the Delfonics and Keith Sweat, "I Wanna Go Outside In the Rain," cause I don't want you to see me cry these tears of "Joy and Pain." Plus sweetheart, "Can you Stand the Rain?"

Cause I can go "On and On." You will never tell me that "Love Shoulda Brought You Home" last night. Shoulda been with me. Because, I was. Erika Badu can pick up Natalie Cole on a "White Horse" and that wouldn't be as "Unforgettable" as the bond we share. "Friends," how many of us have them? But a "Homie, Lover, Friend," that's so very, very rare. You see your "Body's Callin" for me and I don't see nothing wrong with a little "Bump-N-Grind." So, I keep "Grindin" like the Clipse. Loving the way you "Rock Yo Hips," while I "Rock the Boat" work the middle, work the middle, change positions, and have you changing faces. I ain't "Foolin Around." So "What's the 411," Hun? "I Go To Work" until the job is done. My Chubb Rock sho-nuff "Treat Em' Right." My next "Wifey," you can turn my house into a home my "Sweet Lady" cause you give me "Butterflies." inside with this "Ghetto Love" that we have. Believe me, "I'm Black and I'm Proud," but "I Ain't too Proud to Beg" for what I want. The TLC you show me makes me cry "Waterfalls" like Lenny Williams. Oh, Oh, Oh, Oh, Oh, Oh, Oh, Oh, Oh, Oh, Oooooh ."Cause I Love You." I Need You like "The Air That I Breathe." You make me "Breathe Again" and you're finer than Toni Braxton. Freddie Jackson can sing "You Are My Lady" at our wedding. So, if you ask me "Do You Wanna Ride in my Mercedes Boy" with you and Pebbles? I would "Say Yes." Because, since we've been together, I've had nothing but "Love and Happiness" and "Happy Feelings." And that's why I will always "Treat You

Like a Lady." You give me love, love, love, love "Crazy Love." "I Wish" R. Kelly would try to grab the keys to your "Ignition." I'd leave his ass "Trapped in the Closet" for interfering with our "Fire and Desire." Tank said it best, "I Deserve" a "Black Butterfly" like you. Jodeci said that you are "Forever My Lady" and I know that you cannot "Forget me Nots," my "Angel." You're a "Choosey Lover" that God chose for me. We can take a "Midnight Train to Georgia." "Yeah," I said "Georgia" and "Let it Burn." This is my "Confessions." And if I could have it "My Way," my Beyonce, cause "I'm Drunk In Love" and I want to "Cater to You." I'll pay your "Bills, Bills, Bills" "As Soon as I Get Home" from work. I ain't "No Scrub." I'm just a man in love with a woman. It's "My Prerogative," but I feel like I have no choice it's something about the sound of your voice, my "Sweet Sadie." "You're My Lady." I'm sorry that DeAngelo and Angie Stone couldn't make a happy home, but I'm your "Black Brotha." You're my "Soul Sistah," soul Sistah, and baby I love your "Kiss" and I find myself "Missing You." Whenever we're apart, the clouds cry a "Purple Rain" just to ease the pain until we're back in each other's arms again. On our wedding day, your girlfriends will say "I Pray" for that type of love.

A Birthday Poem for Ronesha

Ronesha,

My love for you is unconditional,

No matter your location- geographical,

From the time of your conception,

I want there to be no misconception,

I love you… even the times you didn't follow my directions,

I'm so proud of your accomplishments.

Through the triumphs and disappointments,

You will always be my baby girl,

And if I could, you know I would give you the world….

And when the world gets tough,

I need you to be tougher,

And always remember you're Beautiful , Strong and

Intelligent,

Just like your mother…

Happy Birthday Ronesha; I Love You!

A Birthday Poem for Nyshayla

Nyshayla, I'm so very proud of you,
In you, I see some of my best attributes,
Besides the physical beauty that you inherently possess
Among them are your intellect, your confidence, and your gallant style of dress.
Your vast number of accomplishments, abounds and exceeds,
Anything I could have hoped for, from one of my seeds,

I'm in awe of the kinetic energy that you have bottled up inside,
Just thinking of the illustrious future that awaits you,
makes me swell up with pride.
This is something that I can't hide, nor do I care to,
I want to shout it from the mountain tops,
and tell the world all about you.

Nyshayla Monique Williams, you are forever
my "Shyla-Wayla,"
Yesterday, tomorrow, and especially todaya, LOL.
And babygirl, no matter your destination on this planet
I will always love you and you can etch that in granite!
Happy Birthday Nyshayla!

Happy Birthday Mama

Today, I want to say Happy Birthday to my Mama,
Throughout my years of heartache and drama,
A woman who has done more than give birth to me,
She has continued to love me unconditionally.

The way that God loves us,
You told us to watch who we trust,
That love has simply been reflected,
how you love me and my brother,
I couldn't have asked for a better teacher or mother.

I want to thank you for the sacrifices that you've made,
And also, for the words of love and encouragement
that you gave,
For those things, I am eternally grateful,
To have you still active in my life… I am so very thankful.

Mama, I wish that I could make every day
feel like your birthday and give presents.
Unfortunately, I'm away on vacation right now and can't
even grace you with my presence.

But that doesn't mean I don't love you,
cause mama, you know I do,
I want to tell you Happy Birthday,
and that I'm always thinking of you!

Happy Birthday Mama. I love you!

How Do I Say Goodbye
Tribute to Reggie Spiller, "Big Reg"

How do I say goodbye to a true friend like you?
I'll do it with style and grace, just like I know you would do,
Your smile brightens up any room that you would walk in,
And to just say that you were a good person, simply won't do, my friend.
Your kind words of encouragement, your generosity,
and award-winning personality,
As a friend, husband, and father
there's no comparing your loyalty.
From young kids to grown men,
you always remained the same,
No matter how successful you got, you never ever changed.
You always had a wisdom about you,
that was far beyond your years,
And in so many ways I looked up to you, even though
we grew up as peers.
You were a beast on the football field and a gentle giant
in real life,
I want you to know that you will truly be missed,
you left a tremendous void in a number of lives,
But now heaven has a new angel,
this is something I am sure of,

Your loved ones have a guardian angel,

with you looking down from above.

I used to yell, "Big Reg" and wait to hear your humble reply.

I'm getting my life right, so I can see you in heaven,

And I'll never have to say Goodbye…. I love you Big Reg!

Can I Get That Chance

Damn girl, you have something that intrigues me,
A pretty face, banging body, but your "convo"
is what got me.
I'm sorry, I must apologize, because I made the crucial
mistake of judging a book by its cover;
And Oh, what a fine cover it is!
But let me get down to biz,
And let me formally make your acquaintance,
So I can begin to keep your love maintenance,
Thru our verbal interaction you've quenched
an insatiable desire that I've longed for,
And from my dealings,
most girls built like you were simply nothing but whores,
Or at least I treated them as such, because after talking to
them there was nothing left but lust,
And trust me, I wanted to be different, I swear it,
But after one dinner date, it was so transparently apparent,
That we had nothing in common more than the physical,
No morals or values and limited capacity from her mental,
Just idiot indulgence in who's trapping the hardest,
Reciting a Ghetto Forbe's List about whose chips go the
farthest.
That would let me know that we were on two
different agendas,
So, I'd temporarily play pretender just to tap that tender,

But, I'm done with that life… I'm in search of a wife,
And from the looks of things, that's going to be you.
You've brought something to the table
that I don't want to lose:
Grown woman qualities and intelligent wifey attributes.
So, I can only hope that the feeling is mutual,
That I've piqued your interest.
Because, until I make you mine, I will get no rest,
Restless nights I'll take in stride,
Until we stand hand in hand, with you as my bride.
Once again, I must apologize for getting ahead of myself,
But, the passion you've awakened in me, I just can't help.
Plus, the lady-like way that you carry yourself,
It's more than a breath of fresh air,
It's more like helium, cause, you got me floating on air.
I'm head over heels for you,
and it's for what's inside your noggin,
Not the head that requires slobbin' and head bobbin',
Although, I'd love to partake in that activity,
I'll most definitely reciprocate,
You got me salivating just thinking about your taste.
And when I flicker my tongue across your clit,
it won't be a waste of time,
As you whimper and whine,
while you arch that spine in ecstasy,
But before we indulge, I need you to stand next to me,
Seeing eye to eye, two stories intertwining

with the same plot,

Stimulating brain waves, the real "G" spot.

Enticing all of me, from my mental to my genitals,

And everything in between,

I want to make you my lady, my wife, and my Queen.

So, without further adieu, in this circumstance,

I just wanna know, can I get that chance?....

An Ohio DRC Experience

Dear Lord, I'm praying for peace in a place of chaos,
I'm so tired of standing in line for the phone and JPay Kiosk,
It's no wonder some of these dudes are locked up,
Because some are mentally ill,
Waiting anxiously in the dayroom,
To hear the C.O.'s call for their pills,
Left to deal with this madness,
Brings on a very deep sadness,
Along with the frustration of the microwave use,
Idiots cooking 30-minute meals; microwave abuse.
I have two workout, 2 or 3 times a day;
just to maintain my sanity,
Or be reduced to sit on my rack;
to deal with all this calamity.
Guys from the same state, claiming their different cities,
Overlooking that we're all in the same predicament,
what a real pity.
Some guys claiming sets and gangs,
Feeling like they need their protection,
Isolating themselves with their so-called peers
And instant segregation.
Waking up to a sea of nonsense,
To me it makes absolutely no sense,
These so-called gangstas and thugs,
Breath smelling like shit; that's why they keep a mean mug,

Claiming they was out there gettin' it,

But when store-day come, they ain't gettin' shit,

Talkin' bout they owe fines or they money ain't hit yet,

What-the-fuck-ever!

They could've been on America's Dumbest Criminals,

But still think their clever,

Steady panhandling in prison,

Claim to be hustlas but the hustle in them is missin',

Claim to be straight,

But some are catchin' and pitchin.'

Damn! This shit is crazy.

It leaves me scratchin' my head,

How was you maken' it rain in da clubs,

And don't even know how to make a bed?

Dear Lord, I pray that your Holy Spirit watches over me,

But this is all part of my experience in the Ohio DRC….

Don't Worry

I've decided not to worry about things I can't control,
All the worry and all the stress has surely taken a toll,
On me, as well as my family,
Concerned about my wellbeing and my physical safety,
Sometimes I think about how my children
will get their next meal,
Or how the woman that I love will maintain her bills,
I know my family has their own lives,
and I don't want to be a distraction,
But I don't want them to forget about me
during my time of absence,
I certainly don't want to be selfish
and make this all about me,
I understand that time can get away from you,
especially when you free,
I wonder if my children will forget our bond
we used to share,
Or will they think because I'm not around,
that I don't even care,
That's simply not the case… I didn't mean to catch this case,
And to be sent away to face all this time,
which is simply just a waste.

I want my family to know I love them,

But I can't worry about things that are out of my control,

I'm letting go and letting God,

Because he's the one who's really in control.

Missing You

I'm missing you more than words can express,
My days, nights, and my soul are filled with an emptiness,
During this time apart, my heart has a void,
And upon my return home, we'll both be overjoyed!
Because baby I'm missing you…
(Missing You)
Baby, I'm missing you; like a warm day in the wintertime,
Everyday, thoughts of you constantly fill my mind,
The love that I have for you has continually grown,
Because of the love & loyalty towards me that you've continually shown,
There's no other woman in this world that I'd rather be with,
And that is why, I want you to know, that you are truly being missed. Baby I miss you!
(Thinking of You)
I want you to know how much you mean to me.
Your letters, kind words, and your loyalty.
I need you to know that your friendship is priceless,
There's no way I could repay you for the love you've shown and your kindness,
My feelings have grown,
because of the qualities you've shown,
I'm compelled to express my feelings for you.
That's why I'm writing this poem,
because I am thinking of you!

The Question

Young man, What are you doing?
Start to really think about the choices you are choosing.
You may think it's cool to hang on the corners, sell drugs, and tote guns,
But when you're laying in the morgue, hospital, or prison, does that sound like fun?
You have your whole life ahead of you;
if you just learn how to act,
Instead of being influenced by rap videos
to go pick up a pack,
You see those video vixens
and those cars are rented.
Those are really glorified illusions, not real-life images.
Some of those same rappers that you look up to
have even went to college,
But they'd rather speak about their acquired wealth
instead of their acquired knowledge.
Try to break the cycle, be a strong link in a weak fence,
Don't become a product of your environment and let that be your defense,
You don't have to join the army to be all that you can be,
Finish high school, enroll in college, and elevate yourself mentally.
If you dream big, then your reality becomes bigger!
What are you going to do?

Happy April Fool's Day

You don't have to be born on April 1st
to be considered a fool,
You can be born at any time of the year,
just look at some of the things you do,
Acting foolish is a choice,
And that's what some people choose,
And it's even more of a crying shame,
When talented people ignore their God given tools,
We've all been given free will,
But that gift is truly priceless
To knowingly do harm to someone,
when your heart is filled with righteousness.
 A Blatant contradiction,
While drugs and alcohol can alter your mind state,
Make you think you're feeling great;
While your brain cells dissipate one at a time,
That's an extremely alarming rate,
While snorting or injecting poison in your body,
You're sealing your own fate.
Destroying your own family,
while yourself you slowly kill,
Spending money with the dope man
that should be spent on paying bills.

Family heroes hooked on heroin.
You're more concerned with self-gratification,
so you ain't caring.
Track-marked arms scar your body,
Unapologetically and Unashamed at who's staring,
To you I say, Happy April Fool's Day
Although, it could be anytime of the year,
I pray that your family finds comfort
While at your funeral, they shed tears…
                Happy April Fool's Day!

My Responsibilities as a Man

It's not limited to my physical strengths

and emotional weaknesses,

My arrogant ways or my humble meekness,

Because in order to be there for my family and provide,

I must be selfless and put all of my pride to the side,

To be whatever they need, in their time of need

Not to be selfish in deeds

and think about my own personal greed.

As the head of the family, I have to be able to think

Not be overly influenced by drugs or the alcohol that I drink,

My responsibility, as a man, is to be a comforter,

To teach my kids right from wrong and to be a nurturer,

To show them unconditional love and be their protector,

To be a shining example to my son, a hero to him

And to show my beautiful daughters

how a man is supposed to treat them.

And to my wonderful, adoring wife,

To be the partner that she needs

to make things easier in her life.

There are a lot of things in this world

that might not go as planned,

But you can rest assured, beyond a shadow of a doubt,

That I will always live up to my responsibilities as a man….

Revolving Door

Let me paint a mental picture for you,

As clear as Aquafina being poured over a window pane;

With imagery so vivid

It might cause you to cry tears from the pain.

Repetitive, revolving doors,

Ensure that they will see us again,

Probation, parole, and this thing they call PRC,

An extension of a jail sentence,

Handed down from the Ohio DRC.

A tangled spider web maze,

A sticky rat trap to leave you in an anger-filled daze.

They say it's designed to keep you

on the straight and narrow,

But because of trumped up charges,

I've had to plea to felonies

that have left my path so very narrow,

I now know why the caged bird sings,

Because I'm now the sparrow,

I'm left feeling sorrow for my tomorrow,

I've been betrayed by my yesterday,

So, upon my release,

I have no choice, but to act like a beast,

That's been brought back,

To his natural habitat,

Left to pillage and scavenge just to stay alive,

A situation so sad, it brings tears to my eyes.

And they wonder why I walk around with a chip on my shoulder,

As big as a boulder,

A flame reduced to ash and now I smolder,

A smoke-filled anger has consumed me,

Especially, when I realize what I've been reduced to.

In the eyes of this society,

A jail-bird or ex-con,

They never look at my pros; only at my cons,

And this is where the revolving door cycle begins,

Fed up with my poverty in this democracy.

I decide to make my struggle end,

Forced back into what I did best,

Drug trafficking to relieve the financial stress,

And that's just what the system wants me to do,

Broken down to my very last compound,

It's the only choice left to choose,

At least that's what most of us think; while inside the box,

But to beat the repeat offender game,

we have to think outside the box,

We have to pave a new road to success,

To create our own lanes,

Or face the disappointment of rejection along with the shame,

Develop a skill-set; Take up a trade or vocational training
Or be reduced to menial labor jobs,
Like toilet cleaning and other things demeaning.
The system is designed for us to fail,
Set up for us to live in hell, once released from jail,
But I refuse to be a victim,
Caught up in the "Catch 22" of the system,
I'm making a conscious decision to use my brain,
All of my positive planning will not be in vain,
I plan to be successful,
Not a failure like they want me to be,
And I will do my part to help close the revolving door,
of the Ohio DRC….

How Can I Trust You

How can I trust you?

Your words are like that of a politician,

Running circles around me like a NASCAR,

And when they stop, they leave skid mark scars on my heart,

It's my own failure for believing in you,

But, you told me you're not like the other girls,

and said I could trust you.

I'm no fool, I can read between the lines,

When I call, sometimes you greet me differently,

One of the tale-tell signs.

It makes me angry when I think about,

You could've just told me the truth,

There's no way that you could think this is "cool",

Having your cake and eating it too.

I have comfort in knowing that karma is a muthafucka,

And all the sheisty things you've done will happen to you

Just like you played a brotha.

I should have gone with my better judgment

and broke up with your ass,

Instead of trying to hold on to you

well after our season was passed.

I'm letting you know that I'm cool,
And that I'm done fuckn' with you,
Cause what happens in the dark,
Always comes to light,
So, how can I every trust you?!

Polish Up

It's time y'all! It's time to Polish up!
While they have us warehoused in a military
barrack-style warehouse,
It's time to Polish-up!
So, don't worry yourselves about the two small flat screens
that they have in the dayrooms,
Be more concerned about getting in the limited programs
they have, or in somebody's classroom,
Because it's time to Polish-up!
Don't even think about how they have grown men sleeping
on twin beds, stacked on-top of each other,
Think about the wisdom you have to give,
And pass it on to one of these
Younger brothas, cause it's time to Polish-up!
Don't complain about the food in the chow-hall
that they serve,
Like you're getting a raw deal.
Think about the "Homeless Folks" that would be happy to
receive these (3) square meals.
It's time to Polish-up!
Don't be so quick to hop on the phone,
just to complain and whine,
Sit back and devise a plan to succeed.
Once you're done doing your Time,
It's time to Polish-up!

Don't be so fast to get on the "JPay" to download music that
clouds your judgment and value system,
Instead, retrospectively think on your life, and make some
corrections so you won't return back to the system.
It's time to Polish-Up!
And if you really can't hear the words I'm saying to you
in a positive light,
Then, it's really time for you to make
some corrections in your life,
And it's time for you to Polish-Up!

The Spirit of Discontent

Some people just have hate in their hearts,
A dark cloud of negative energy.
Just waiting to rain on anybody's parade,
C.O.'s bringing their own personal issues to work,
Only to make some inmates lives a living hell,
Like the hell they constantly live in,
Judges deciding the fates of the accused,
Basing their judgment off of how well their nights went
If their lustful desires aren't fulfilled,
then jail cells they'll fill,
Police officers walking around with a chip on their shoulder,
Because of being bullied in high school.
Now, they jump at every opportunity
to flex their muscle of authority.
Case managers hide behind grumpy facades.
Why would you take a job that requires you to interact with people if you're not a people person?
Now, I'm not saying that all these people
have hate in their hearts,
But, some do possess the spirit of discontent,
Not happy with the current state of their own lives.
They purposely sabotage anyone else's happiness that they can, and for these people I pray,
I pray that God gives them peace in their lives,
and open their eyes,
So that they can see the error of their ways....

Jesus Paid the Price

For the whole world's sins,
He gave his life.
All you have to do is believe,
and eternal life you will receive,
Because of the Lamb of the World's sacrifice,
we now have salvation,
Simply, because Jesus paid the price….

What Happened?

Whatever happened to feel good music?
I must be getting old,
because it's hard for me to relate to today's music,
Most of the songs do nothing to lift us up.
All it does is get people amped up and turned up,
A lot of the youth want to live out the life of the music lyrics,
They turn into the glorified characters every time they hear it.
We need more music of substance; not just music that
glorifies abuse of a substance,
Bob Marley, Marvin Gaye, and Stevie Wonder painted
pictures with their lyrics,
Music that not only could you feel, but you could also see it,
Now don't get me wrong, I see glimpses of what music could
be in some songs,
But the percentages are so small;
it makes me not want to listen to it at all,
The most popular artists have the biggest platform;
But they don't use it,
And it still leaves me to ask the question,
What happened to the feel-good music?

Testimony: Part 1

I feel like I'm being tested,

In my life; unfavorable situations have manifested,

But, my faith is still unwavering.

This is one of those times,

not to lean on my own understanding,

Because I know that God has a plan for me,

And now that I've given my life to Christ,

the devil just keeps on testing me,

But I continue to smile in the face of adversity.

I'm totally aware that things could be worse for me,

This storm I'm going through will soon pass.

I'm looking forward to the blessings

that are ahead in my path,

I realize that God has allowed me to be tested for a reason,

He wants to see if I will remain faithful

for more than just one season,

And I will: with the greatest resolve.

The issues I'm facing; I know only he can solve,

I pray every day that God keeps showing favor to me,

And I will spread his message to the world thru my testimony....

Testimony : Part 2

It's so frustrating

because it seems like nothing's going right for me,

I'm in a state of confusion,

My ego's been bruised; a vanity confusion,

I must confess that this institutional stress; often leaves me feeling depressed

But you know what, forget about that "Woe is Me" attitude,

I'm now taking on the spirit of gratitude,

Instead of looking at the glass as half-empty,

I'm going to look at it as half-full,

It's time to put some pep in my step, without the Red-bull,

I want to thank God for his grace and mercy,

Because I could be a lot worse off,

I have my health to be thankful for,

While others can't get rid of a cough,

I have complete control over my mental faculties,

While others are being housed in mental facilities,

I'm so grateful to still have my mother and father still alive,

While others visit theirs in the cemetery

and can't help but to cry,

When I look at my life thru a microscope

I now see things so much clearer,

Like how I've truly been blessed.

I feel the presence of God is near
And when I start to feel like I'm getting frustrated,
Like nothing's going right for me,
I will now smile thru these tests,
Because I know that it's just a part of my testimony…

When I Fell in Love With You

As I lay on my rack, I backtrack in my mind,
To find the exact time, to remember when I fell in love.
It was a brisk cool late fall night,
And you and I were taking flight,
Off a loud blunt I had just twisted,
Fresh off work,
I was counting the proceeds from my daily business.
And I was still coming up short of the bills that were due
You saw the anguish on my face and said,
"What's wrong Papi, what can I do?"
I was too ashamed to ask for help,
so instead I shook my head,
You looked at me with that pretty face and said,
"Closed mouths don't get fed."
I already had deep feelings
and was most definitely feeling you,
And don't get me wrong when I say this cause the amount
you offered me was more than cool,
But it was at that exact moment that I knew,
Based solely off that very simple fact,
I knew that you were going to always have my back,
And you were going to love me back
the way that I would love you.

Your love and loyalty transcend this earthly realm

This is something I feel compelled to tell,

To the world, but to especially you,

My sweet loving and kind Darling Boo.

The way that we both love has been reciprocated,

And not to make things too complicated,

God has merely duplicated.

The way we both love

and placed this inside both me and you,

So, as I lay back on my rack and backtrack in my mind,

Just to find the exact time,

when I fell in love with you,

That particular moment stands out.

Without a shadow of a doubt,

But, as sure as the sun rises and clear skies are blue,

I believe that God has allowed me to go thru this situation,

just so I could truly appreciate you….

What is My Purpose?

I often ask the question, "What is my purpose?"

Am I on a self-serving mission?

Or should I live a life of public service?

Well, just like time heals all wounds,

It also has a way of sorting out things.

Thru my life's trials and tribulations,

My path has been altered, under God's "directioning"

With my heart as my moral compass,

As I navigate thru this wilderness,

Stumbling across predestined destinations,

With love and tenderness.

Conquering contempt thru conversation,

Dismantling disputes by the droves,

Establishing esteem with examination,

Forming the framework for fortune; watching a story unfold.

Words don't have to be spoken

for the message to be heard loud and clear.

Just be still and know that God is God,

And bask in his presence that's near....

I'm Back

I'm back y'all, I've come back to society,

And where some may say, well he was just away,

At jail, prison, and even the penitentiary,

In some respects, you're right,

Although, it didn't feel like it to me,

Because I've been remolded and refined,

while in God's refinery,

My transgressions of yesterday are directly related to my triumphs of tomorrow,

Because in order to be at this place of peace in my life,

I had to experience some sorrow,

I've embraced that pain

in order for me to be able to love again.

But this time with a sincere heart,

And the next time I find love,

I won't be so quick to let it fall apart,

By being self-absorbed and also selfish,

I'll be more attentive to her needs,

constantly offering her help,

Selflessly loving my woman

instead of just worrying about myself.

During my extended stay vacation,

I now have a greater appreciation,

for this affectionate situation,

So, like I said y'all, I'm back in society,

But, I wasn't just doing time, or letting time do me,

I was busy being refined in God's precious refinery....

Waiting for my 1ˢᵗ Visit

Anticipating and awaiting your arrival,
I want to hop on the phone
just to make sure you're still coming,
But, I don't want to cause you distraction
while you're driving.
Or, frustrate you with my lack of patience,
so, I wait.
I wait until I hear my name or bed number
called by the 1ˢᵗ shift C.O.'s
Letting me know that you have arrived
safely to your destination,
The phone rings and I wait,
I wait to hear them call for me, West 94!
Damn, that's not me!
I, go to the officer's desk just to verify,
"Excuse me Sir, did you call West 34?"
"No, I called West 94"…
 "Ok, I was just checking."
I say with a forced smile as to not agitate the C.O.
And so, I wait,
I go back to the dayroom and wait,
I wait to hear the phone ring again,
Listening to the miscellaneous conversations that irritate me
so much,

The coughing, the hacking up of phlegm, only to be swallowed again,

The escalating volume to talk about nothing continues,

And I continue to wait,

I wait in silence, deafen by my thoughts

The phone rings again, and I wait.

"Yard Open!" Yells the C.O.;

"Damn!" (I say in my frustration and I wait),

I grab a book and go use the bathroom,

Because the nervousness gave me bubble guts, LOL.

I wash my hands,

upon finishing and exiting the restroom.

When I come out, someone says,

"I think the C.O. is looking for you."

I smile, because I know my girl has just arrived,

And I know I'm about to get my first visit…

New-Age Slavery

I've been kidnapped,
Taken as a captive by slave traders posing as police officers,
Whisked off to a holding place, known as the county jail.
With no intention of freeing me, I receive no bail,
I bide my time, waiting for my turn to appear,
In front of a judge, who will decide my fate,
the new-age slave auctioneer.
Even my "sales rep," known as my lawyer,
has more control than me in this situation,
As I stand nervously in the courtroom,
Slave Trade block to hear the time duration
that I will spend in their prison system,
a fancy name for a plantation,
They call it the department of corrections,
Well, they need to correct that title
to the department of warehousing-
Prison blues being the new black,
Grown men crammed in dormitory housing,
Disconnected from my family.
Isolated from the rest of society,
Birthdays pass as just another day,
The joyful meanings have been stripped away
from once celebrated holidays.

Desolate days have left me a shell of the man I used to be,
As a result, I'm emotionally dysfunctional.
Once I am finally set free;
Holding grudges against family and so-called friends
who didn't reach out for me,
Employment opportunities are limited,
Ostracized, because of my criminal history,
Structureless days fill my calendar,
As I am left to fend for me,
All because I was kidnapped,
And taken captive away from society.

Rest in Peace Sistah Maya

"Rest in Peace," Sistah Maya,
You have fought the good fight,
With the social consciousness of your poetry,
You've inspired generations of poets to write,

With the book, "I Know Why the Caged Bird Sings"
You spoke to many hearts,
Just like the great Dr. Martin Luther King,
You were a hero to a race of people whose skin is dark,

And then, the deep piece, "Still I Rise,"
You gave others the will to persevere,
So, with Barack as our President; to me it's no surprise,
As our oppressor's land we commandeer,

So, rest in peace, "Sistah Maya"
And I use that term with great reverence,
With each and every poem that I write,
I will try to capture the spirit of your essence….

Mothers, Daughters, and Sistahs

Let me speak life into some young woman who feels she hasn't yet reached her stride,

You are the backbone of nations;

So, hold your head up with pride,

Your nurturing nature has cultivated kings,

Presidents, dignitaries, among other things,

Young ladies, wipe away the tears,

Never feel sorry for yourselves,

Don't accept any type of abuse from anyone,

Know your human wealth,

Young girls, respect your body,

Because you only get just one,

Don't be tricked into losing your innocence,

By the slick tongue of one of our sons,

Young mothers, to our future you hold the key,

You must instill values and morals in our children,

To increase their odds to succeed,

Young daughters, stay proud,

But practice humility,

Remember that you reap the rewards of what you sow,

In the fields of this treacherous society,

Young sistahs, prepare yourselves,

To carry on a legacy,

Of young slave girls tossed overboard in their journey.

Their legacies lost at sea,

Nubian Queens, you are the mother to all of civilization,

So, pick up your cross; to release your sins,

And on each other please stop Hatin'....

Black Girls Rock!

Nervous

I'm uneasy, but I try to remain calm,

My throat is dry, but I'm still sweating from my palms,

I feel nauseous, my stomach is queasy,

But nothing comes up, I guess I'm dry heaving,

My thoughts race with no finish line,

So many scenarios invade my mind,

I start to speak, but nothing comes out,

And when the words do finally escape my mouth,

I begin to babble,

Searching for words that make sense,

Like I'm playing scrabble,

This is not my typical behavior,

And I certainly don't deserve this,

But this is something we've all experienced

by just simply being nervous….

Fight the Power

I'm no Flavor Flav or Chuck D,
But it's gonna take a nation of millions to hold me back,
I'm the new Public Enemy,
That's why I will continue to fight the powers that be,
A conscious black man trying to enlighten my people,
Well, that's something they don't want to see,
Instead of putting firearms in their hands,
I want to arm them with a very successful plan,
Because, the school system only pacifies;
not emphasize the importance of knowledge,
They say don't leave any child behind,
But they're not properly equipping our children for college,
The thirst for learning should begin early in life,
With mom and dad supplying the canteen
To quench that thirst for knowledge,
As parents, it's our duty to prepare our children
for this world in which we live,
Video games are not the answer,
but it's the most frequent gift that we give,
And this social media generation
can't keep anything discrete,
They tweet and Instagram everything they do;
even the food that they eat.

We live in a society where mass shootings
happen on a daily basis,
Seems like the world's gone crazy;
right before our faces,
War veterans can't receive proper health care,
Selfies and self-destructive images captivate our stares,
And we can't look away; a beautify tragedy,
Fuck a Justin Bieber.
Look at the transformations of a Will Smith
or a Queen Latifah,
And let that be our blueprint; with their talents being
amplified thru dedication and hardworking time spent,
Like I said, I'm no Flavor Flav or Chuck D,
But it's gonna take a nation of millions to hold me back,
I'm the new Public Enemy,
That's why I will continue to fight the power that be,
A conscious black man trying to enlighten my people,
Well, that's just something they don't want to see….

Ossie and Ruby Dee

Ossie Davis and Ruby Dee were American Treasures,
forgiving thru the midst of racial turmoil
beyond the realm of measure.
Thru our social tribulations, they continued to surge on,
Leaving a legacy for future generations,
to look encouragingly upon.
Their quintessential romance was the epitome of black love,
As pure and perfect as the clear blue sky
that we gaze at up above,
Their kindred spirits displayed luminously,
while on the silver screen,
They also served as Masters of Ceremony
for the famous Dr. King Jr. speech, "I Have a Dream."
Even before that Ossie's eloquent articulation
eulogized our fallen brother Malcolm X,
And at 84 years old, Ruby received an Oscar nomination
for best supporting actress,
Individually and collectively
their accolades we're more than just a few,
but more importantly,
the template of their relationship is something to aspire to.
Ossie was laid to rest first,
and now Ruby Dee has passed on,
But your shining example
of true black love will continue to luminate on....

Fed up

I'm so tired of seeing my children grow up
through pictures along a timeline,
While I sit alone in a jailcell,
or in a crowded prison dormitory; doing hard time.
I was once blinded by dollar signs; but now I have sight,
I now know what true wealth is;
and that is being a part of my children's lives,
I've missed birthdays, holidays, and also graduations.
But despite my obvious absence; my children have still
furthered their education.
A true testament to their own perseverance,
Not letting my elongated confinement
cause them interference,
The undeniable blood of my forefathers
passed on to my seeds,
Forgiving thru any obstacles
until they ultimately succeed,
The untamable spirit of African Warriors
that were cast away at sea,
Have manifested themselves in me;
and I've passed them onto my offspring,
Uncage-able birds soaring and flying high,
Not letting constraints of this land,
Limit their exploration of the vast worldly sky….

Looking for Love in All the Wrong Places

I've been looking for love in all the wrong places,

Searching in nightclubs and bars staring at drunk faces,

Somehow finding them attractive,

in my alcohol induced oasis,

Wasted time spent;

in relationships that dead-end like cul-de-sacs,

Frivolous years spent with people that could do nothing

but hold me back,

Looking passed the fact that we were unequally yoked,

To think that we would work was nothing more than a joke,

But I will have the last laugh,

I'm moving forward towards my destiny,

Wiser from the lessons learned from my past,

The person that I want to spend my life with,

We must be mentally and physically compatible,

Not disagreeing all the time about small things,

Constantly engaging in verbal battles,

The person who I want to spend my life with,

We must have common views and interests,

We'll be attentive to each other's needs and also selfless,

I'm praying that God sends me that homie-lover-friend,

And one day this exhausting search will eventually end,

Because I've been looking for love in all the wrong places....

The Company You Keep

They say if you want to know who you are,
just look at the company that you keep,
And when you look around yourself are you completely
satisfied with what you see,
Chances are only a small percentage
will be there thru thick and thin,
While multitudes will flock to your side
when you're victorious in a win,
But when the chips are down;
fair-weather friends blow you off like tumbleweed,
They quickly forget, how you were there for them
in their time of need,
Selective amnesia is what I call it;
or it could be considered a character flaw,
Something that when choosing my friends;
I should have saw.
But I'm not perfect by any means;
just like the friends that I kept,
I should've peeped some of their selfish ways
and realized that we are skept.
Is that one of the reflections of me?
One of my character flaws under reciprocation,
If so, I want to remove that part of me;
call it a character flaw castration.

If I'm judged by the company I keep,

respect, loyalty, and integrity I must display,

Soaring with comrades of similar qualities

as the Golder Rules we obey,

Fair-weather friends come a dime a dozen;

I need real friends that can stand rain,

We'll be there for each other thru the triumphs and the pain,

So, the next time I face judgment by the company that I keep,

I will smile at the persecutors because my friends will be a

true reflection of me....

My Legacy

What kind of legacy will you leave behind?
Will it be the hustle and bustle of your job,
While you're on your daily grind,
Most likely not, but most of us don't stop,
To smell the roses, so to speak,
Placing emphasis on things that are so oblique,
Unparalleled and incomparable to what's really essential,
The consequential formative bonds of being parental,
The framework to our family structure,
Being positive role-models;
more than just a father and mother,
While showing reverence to our creator,
Teaching responsibility and accountability,
Acting dignified, but showing wholehearted humility,
And when my life is looked back upon in retrospect,
I don't want one of the glorified qualities
of my existence to be neglect,
For my family or my fellow man,
But for my candor and issues, that I was passionate about,
And my willingness to enlighten the less conscious man,
For my introverted personality, and my charitable deeds,
As I extended my helping hand, to assist those in need.

And last, but certainly not least,
My abundant love for my family,
My protective nature, ensuring their safety and security,
That's what I want my legacy to be.
What kind of legacy will you leave behind?

Are You Who I've Prayed For

Are you the one, who I've prayed to God for?
Because, I'm so tired of dealing with loose women
and self-proclaimed whores,
Wearing masquerades of virtuousness,
I'm simply asking these questions,
due to your perfect timeliness,
You came into my life, at just the right time.
Giving me a glimpse of hope,
when my heart's eyes had turned blind,
Unfulfilled promises have left me emotionally scared,
My dreams of a righteous woman,
have been undoubtedly marred,
And then you come into my life,
with grandiose notions of becoming my wife,
What feels like out of the seemingly blue,
But I believe your intentions and motives are
unconventionally true,
So, I thank God that you came into my life at this time,
And only time will tell if it's for a reason,
A season, or for a lifetime…

Let Me In

Baby let me in,
Let me inside your mind,
cause I feel inclined to help you,
It's so obvious you have some blind spots,
Especially from my point of view,
I need to alter some things inside of you,
To give you a full panoramic angle of view,
I want to enhance your rudimentary qualities,
As a person, parent, and spouse.
And to let anyone take advantage of you,
Well, that's something that I can't allow.
I've grown fond of some of the features that you possess,
And I won't allow anyone to bring you down,
Or cause you unnecessary stress,
Excuse me for having a heart,
but I protect those whom I care about,
This is something you need to understand about me,
Beyond any shadow of a doubt,
Since you've allowed me in; and asked me to be your King,
I'm expecting you to know your place;
And always act like a Queen....

Love

Love is supposed to be patient and kind,
It's not supposed to have me going crazy
out of my mind,
Love is supposed to be supportive and understanding,
Love's not supposed to be selfish and demanding,
That's not love; but some other characteristic,
Love should be positive and optimistic;
not negative and pessimistic.
And if love is not making you feel joy and happiness,
Not pain and sadness,
Well, that's not love anymore.
Some other sentiment has walked thru love's door,
Please don't be fooled or misconstrued,
By some other emotion disguised as love
that makes you feel used,
That emotion could be lust,
Having you falling deeper in it;
With each pump and each thrust,
Trust me; I've been there,
Sweaty, sticky, hot passion; once had me ensnared,
That feeling could be infatuation or admiration,
But that's still not an invitation to neglect me,
Love is supposed to respect me; not disrespect me,
Love is supposed to encourage me; not discourage me,
For pursuing my hopes and dreams,

Love's supposed to build me up;

Not tear down my self-esteem,

I know that love can hurt;

but it shouldn't be synonymous with pain,

Love shouldn't make me ask the question,

Do I ever want to love again?

Because love can be exhausting

and invigorating at the same time,

So, I hope and pray, that love comes my way,

And God directs my path, so true love I will find…

Thank God for My Problems

Let me try to explain,
How I embrace the pain in my life,
My brother, I don't need any tissue,
Cause I'm thanking God for my issues,
Sometimes God has to sit you down by yourself,
In a place where you can't depend on nobody,
And you can't ask for more help.
Where all you can do is call on him,
So, I wanna thank God for my issues and my problems,
I thank God for giving me a chance to restore
and renew my faith,
When things don't always happen fast,
Sometimes you got to wait,
And during that time my God is working on me,
Like Marvin Sapp said, "He Saw the Best in Me,"
But I had too many people around to see my own reflection,
He had to isolate me, so he could change my life's direction,
So, I wanna thank God for my problems & my struggles,
I wanna thank God for allowing me to get in this trouble,
Because in the eye of the storm; I now see my purpose,
And all of my issues,
problems and struggles were surely worth it,
My God is continually molding me,
Into a poet, an author, and a soldier in his army,
And for this; I thank God for me problems!

I Know I've Been Changed

Oh Lord, I know I've been changed,

To my haters, it might sound strange,

To the nay-sayers; I might sound crazy and deranged,

But Oh Lord, I know I've been changed,

I don't react to things the way I use to react,

And I don't act how I use to act,

Although my personality may have some theatrics in it,

I'm closer to a saint, than I am a sinner.

Oh Lord, I know I've been changed,

I don't run with the folks; I use to run with,

And although I'm far from perfect,

I'm now living life with a purpose,

Oh Lord, I know I've been changed,

I don't even think how I use to think,

Lord knows,

 I don't drink how I used to drink,

I no longer smoke and take my life as a joke,

Oh Lord, I know I've been changed….

I'm Ashamed of Some of Our Black Men

I live in a world, with a black man as president
of the most powerful nation,
I'm so very proud of him,
but that's just the start of this conversation,
Because there are so many of our black men
that I can be ashamed of,
Some of the ones that make their change
off of calling our sistahs names,
The ones that don't make an effort to change
and use the white man as their blame,
When they don't even know what real struggle is,
Struggles like watching your kids being sold in front of you,
Struggles like hearing your women being raped
just out of your view,
Struggles like "Putting on the Face" of "Yes Sir Boss!"
Biting your tongue to the point that blood is almost lost,
Real struggles for which our forefathers died,
And these young dudes don't even have enough pride,
To pull up their pants or pick up their feet when they walk,
Not enough pride to even annunciate when they talk.

And that's just a small part of their ways,

Quick to make a baby, but won't stay around to help raise,

Won't even pay child support; but say they gettin' paid,

And they have the nerve to call themselves a man,

Well, they wouldn't know a real man

if they were standing next to one,

They'd probably think he was a square;

if he didn't say, "You know what I mean son!"

I'm convinced that ignorance is their defense,

But it still doesn't stop me from

being ashamed of some of our so-called black men…

Epiphany

I've had an epiphany of sorts,
So, allow me to share the symphony of serendipity,
And I won't retort,
My statements, comments, or observations.
I'm so concerned with the state of our Black Nation,
Young black men overlooking their obligations,
And our young sistahs obliging their degradation,
We have some serious issues on our hands,
Being hung by the psychological nooses
of the music we choose
No longer is it the so-called "white man,"
"I'm black, but I'm sellin' white!"
"Young nigga move that dope,
young nigga move that dope!"
This must be a joke,
But, they're the ones laughing at our race,
And in the race to succeed;
we're the ones who's falling behind,
Our beautiful brown eyes have become blind,
While lyrical pollution clutters our mind,
And we "jig" to the beat.
Shuckin' and Jivin'' movin' our feet,
Like buffoons to a Willie Lynch tune.

We need to tune out these malicious melodies,

That gives excuses to our young black men to commit multiple felonies,

We need an abrupt cycle disruption,

Cause there's been a major malfunction,

And I'm waiting for change; I'm waiting for an answer,

And I'll continue to wait,

Until I have another epiphany!

Proud of You

I'm so proud of you,

The more my consciousness is awakened,

I'm so very proud of the path you've taken,

In route to learn your blackness,

Immersing yourself totally with no slackness,

The experiences and lessons you've had collegiately,

Can never be replaced,

Just like the dreams you're pursued can never be erased,

My seed has grown, blossomed, and bloomed,

Making your family and real friends proud,

As well as our ancestors encased in Egyptian Tombs,

And I speak for all of us,

When I say we're proud of You!

The Maze of Your Existence

I want to lose myself in the maze of your existence,
There will be no repentance,
Cause, I'm not the least bit sorry for feeling this way,
Nor will I make excuses for your ex's misuses,
Because, he didn't appreciate what he had,
And that's truly the sad part,
That someone born with sight
could simply overlook the precious gift that is you,
You're a Queen, Your Majesty,
And it's more than a travesty
that you're not being treated as such,
With love, respect, and trust,
Cause, that's what I bring to the table,
I tell you no fables,
You don't have to wear any labels
you're not comfortable with.
We can take our time to explore one another,
mentally and physically,
And spiritually well bound
like elements from the periodic table,
Compounding and mixing,
Creating something new for the world to view.

Excuse me if I'm getting too profound,

But baby girl that's just how I get down,

I'm more than just the King that wears the crown,

I'm a man of Renaissance

on the Reconnaissance mission

for reciprocating adulation,

And you're my target,

The bullseye's on your cardiovascular region,

And hunting, then mating season will begin,

I'll be diligent in my persistence,

Just because,

I simply want to lose myself

in the maze of your existence….

Board Game of Love

I don't like to play games,
But baby, I need to have a "Monopoly" on your love,
I'm not looking to collect anything
but your affection and loyalty
When I pass go,
I'll luxury tax that ass and caress your community chest
to the point you'll wanna buy me houses and hotels,
So run tell that,
You'll never have to go directly to jail,
Cause like Kanye, I'll have yo' love locked down,
Hand and hand, we'll skip through this "Candyland",
on a "Trivial Pursuit" of happiness,
I'll be the doctor and you'll be my patient
in this game of "Operation",
I wanna hear you buzz when I hit the sides,
As your legs intertwine in alignment just like "Connect
Four"…You can pour all of your emotions into me,
No illustrations necessary in our love "Pictionary",
But I don't mean to babble, but I'm trying to put the right
words together like "Scrabble",
Simply to express how I feel,
No elementary games like "Checkers";
it's more complex like "Chess",
And I'm trying to stay ahead three steps
in this board game called love.

Why Are You So Mad at Me?

I don't know why you're so mad at me,

Like, all of your hopes and dreams have been dashed by me,

What you need to do is look in the mirror

with your own eyes,

Because unfortunately, you've been the cause

of your own demise,

Carrying baggage from your past

only hinders the travel of future endeavors,

And although you may think it's clever

to call someone names,

It just displays a major character flaw,

You're unable to use restraint or contain your emotions

like a sensible adult,

So, you have to take a jolt at my manhood,

Childish justification to make your own self feel good,

I'm glad that you have showed me the real you so early,

Before I became glued to you for all eternity,

It's truly a shame that you would want to remain encased in

the uncomfortable comfort zone of what you're used to,

Dealing with males that only looked at you

as tail or, at best, as a side piece,

In which to slide their meat,

but never did you meet and greet their families,

You've grown to accept mediocrity,

It was a true hypocrisy for me to treat you with more value

than what you saw in yourself,

And, as for your issues of self-worth,

you really should seek some help,

But that help won't come for me,

nor will I continue to stick around to see you working on you,

I'm totally exhausted and completely done

with your verbal abuse,

I know that I wasn't perfect,

but I tried to treat you like a Queen,

And I'm still left wondering why you're so mad at me….

Life's Doors

Life's door opens and closes at God's Command

It's all part of His divine plan,

It's not meant for us to understand

with our earthly comprehension,

Not to mention, how his division and subtraction

adds up to more than what we have envisioned,

For our own lives and paths

Now you do the math,

And if you want to make God laugh,

Just tell him what you have planned for yourselves,

In your paradise plan, you might have to go thru some hell,

Maybe even in jail you may dwell for a season,

Just to become seasoned enough

to appreciate your God given abilities,

Your source of frustration

could be the pivotal point to help change your life's direction,

That's just how God works in our lives,

And I've been personally privy to the phrase,

"All things work for the good."

It's help me to understand

when things were not always understood.

So, turn this opposition into an opportunity,
Pass this test, so you can testify about God's grace,
And keep a smile on your face
while you display your unwavering faith,
Because this situation is all a part of God's plan,
And just remember that life's door opens
and closes at God's command....

The N-Word

Nigger, nigger, nigger!
Pick that cotton!
Bale that hay!
Nigga, nigga, nigga…
A term of endearment this generation uses today,
To me, it's simply a connotation of humiliation.
Disguised as brotherly admiration,
Nigger, nigger, nigger,
Who's your Massah?
Where's your papers?
Nigga, nigga, nigga,
What set you claim?
How you make that paper?
To me, their seeking a sense of power and unity,
Something that's been absent
or fleeting in our black community,
Nigga, nigga, nigga,
Trying to turn a negative into something positive,
A true testament to the perseverance of our black race,
Whether nigger or nigga,
To me, it doesn't lessen the sting,
I propose the motion
to remove the word from your vocabulary,
So, we can set our future generations free…

The Continuation of the Dream

I have an earnest desire to inspire
no matter what has transpired in my life,
it's my instinct to distinctively ensure
that my people don't
become extinct from this earth,
and, for what it's worth,
I relish at the opportunity to shoulder this burden,
I'm so certain that I was chosen,
appointed and anointed,
For this job slash task
and I will take care of this matter at hand,
Providing inspiration thru enlightenment,
To invigorate and motivate thru acquaint information,
It's my obligation, my duty, and my responsibility,
To teach ethnic pride and Godly humility,
I am the continuation of Dr. King's dream,
Aspirations of justice and equality is what I bring,
And although my swagger is different,
My mission is similar,
Because, I pray for all; not just some,
And I'm anticipating a very positive outcome,

Like Tupac once said,

"I may not be the one who makes a change, but if I can spark

the mind of the one who will, I've done my job."

So, if I can be that Amber of light

to ignite the brain that will bring about change,

Then my mission has been achieved,

And Dr. King's midnight mirage was more than just a dream.

Domestic Violence

Look at what you made me do!
Baby, I'm sorry… I won't do it again,
I don't like it when I have to put my hands on you,
And who was that guy you were talking to?
Baby, I told you he was just a friend,
Where have you been?
You got off from work hours ago!
Baby, I told you I had some errands to run,
Girl, you better watch who the fuck you talking to,
Baby, please don't talk to me like that;
especially not in front of our son,
I don't want you hanging out with your girlfriends,
Them hoes don't mean you no good!
Baby, I grew up with them; they got my back,
You heard what I said; end of discussion understand,
O.K. baby, understood,
See, now look at what you made me do!
Now, go put some make-up on that fucking eye,
Baby, I told him not to call me no more,
You tryn' to play me like a fool;
you can quit tellin' me all them damn lies,

Wait until we get home!
Since you want to embarrass me in public,
Baby, he's a friend of my brother's,
Then, why he trying to hug you and shit?
Baby, please stop;
was one of the final pleas
before her cries fell silent,
And this is just one example
of a dysfunctional relationship,
Full of domestic violence.

Life Lessons

I need to speak to my sistahs for a minute,
I want to talk to each and everyone of you
like one of my own daughters,
And, maybe I can teach you some things
that your mother and father should have taught ya'
You're a beautiful Queen, inside and out,
Never let wonder, uncertainty, or doubt,
Cause your self-esteem to plummet to the depths
of depression,
To the point where you use sex as a weapon
or form of expression,
To give value to yourself
or to gain a man's affection,
Make sure you're the object of his affection
and not just the object of erection,
Never let a relationship be the measurement of your worth,
Never accept anything less than what you deserve,
In this amusement park of life;
remember that you are the prize,
Never oblige the lies told from guys
that don't merit your time,
Don't let someone else's wants eclipse your needs,
Remember, you're the sun in your universe;
a true star indeed,

Don't tolerate any mistreatment

in any fashion,

shape or form,

Don't welcome dysfunction

and embrace it as your norm,

Don't let anyone stop you from pursuing your dreams,

Remember that anything you set out to accomplish

you can achieve,

All you have to do is believe in yourself;

like I believe in you

And to thine own self, always remain true,

Recall, that these are life lessons I've taught

and will teach to my future daughters,

And if you pay attention close enough, you might

learn some lessons that your parents should've taught ya....

Full-Potential

Are you living up to your full-potential?
Or are you an untapped well of latent energy
waiting to be discovered by the explorer known as
ambition?...
Tarrying in a state of stagnation,
Making your color an explanation for your current situation
in a nation that labels itself the land of the free,
Are you saying that, that title doesn't belong to thee,
Someone who's industrious and determined doesn't let
where they are currently define where they are going in life,
As humans, we've all experienced some strife
during our lifetime,
But in the meantime, you persevere;
no matter how severe the adversities may seem,
Don't let anything or anyone stop you
from realizing your dreams,
Haters may say that it sounds far-fetched,
But, if you look at life simply as an etch-a-sketch where you
can create your own reality out of nothing,
Don't allow anybody to shake your hopes away,
Someone who has never been anywhere
will be the first one to offer you directions,
And they would be remised,
if they didn't tell you about their own neglections.

As they reflect on what they once
envisioned for themselves,
So, delve into yourself to find
the purpose of your presence
during this earthly time duration,
And once you find out who you are,
Give yourself an astounding salutation
that's overdue, but ever so essential.
And then, and only then, will you start
living up to your potential…

Still Waters

Still waters run deep,
As deep as the abyss of loneliness,
Causing a vortex of unbearable trauma on one's soul,
I've heard stories; but to experience anguish firsthand,
Insomnia, lack of appetite, feelings of despair & depression,
Just to name a few of the symptoms
of the aftermath of the cataclysmic devastation
of a once thriving and vibrant relationship.
Where did we go wrong?
What could I have done differently?
Is there someone else?
These are some of the most frequently asked questions
after a breakup.
In some cases, there are no concrete answers,
Only more questions….

"My Commentary"

I've been on a radical sabbatical, to say the least,
Maneuvered through a jungle of obstacles
and walked away a beast,
Isolation in obscurity couldn't break my stride,
All it did was fuel my drive like wind currents to a jet stream,
And what the devil thought would break my spirit,
God used to build up my self-esteem,
He turned my opposition into an opportunity,
And from my new perspective, I've had a chance to view,
what's been missing in my community,
Positive role models and grass roots leadership
is just the tip of the iceberg of issues
that plagued my kinship,
Eroding emphasis on education,
Coupled with devoiding values of vocation,
And a total disregard for human animation,
Misguided and mishandled youth are often misunderstood
and mistreated because of a generational gap,
Mistaken for a lack of respect,
Well, how could they have a lack of something
in which they were never trained?

An inexcusable neglection on the behalf of their guardians,
As role models, we have to set better examples,
Providing ample samples of the Golden Rule,
Arming them with a very basic tool for success,
Which is that foundation of respect
As an entire community, we have to do better
And I know that one day
We will get it together…

Pleasure to Meet You

Please excuse this erotic interlude,
But, as your firm nipples protrude thru your shirt,
You got me wondering what's underneath that skirt,
And, by the way you sashay and sway your hips,
like your pussy lips are feathers tickling your inner thighs,
I wouldn't be the least bit surprised if your "love cave"
could turn the average man into a "love slave."
While your pussy whip brothas
like overseers on a southern plantation,
The mere fascination has me salivating while contemplating
what your love nectar must taste like,
Be it pungent or sweet; however, fantastically aromatic,
Your pheromones are an instantaneous aphrodisiac,
Fraternizing with my senses of sensuality,
To you, a commonality, but, to me, a rarity,
Because, never have I met a woman so appeasing to me,
Sorry to be so forward in my initiation of conversation,
But, your appearance and your fragrance has stirred carnal
desires in me that I didn't know existed,
I feel I must be persistent in my pursuit of your company,
My name is Brotha Poet, and yours must be my Queen,
Because that's what I intend to address you as,
As I caress your mental and undress your physical in unison.

Duality at its finest,

But I guess, as a formality,

I must get your number first,

And please know,

that these lines weren't rehearsed or scripted,

As you write down those seven digits for a brotha,

By the way, it's a pleasure to meet you…

When Will It End

Please stop killing our young men, Mr. Policeman,

I thought you were here to protect and serve,

But, when you're around we have to duck and swerve

your billy clubs and bullets,

I thought you had to yell "freeze" first,

Before you had the right to pull it,

I guess I was misinformed

or does your uniform give you the license

to ignore the same laws that you were sworn to enforce,

Of course, this question is rhetorical,

Because, historical facts confirm the worst of our suspicions,

From the southern murders of the 60's,

To the Cincinnati,

and most recently the Ferguson, Missouri Riots,

When will it cease to exist,

I must persist to ask a question

that probably can't be answered in a few sentences,

But, still I'll ask,

If nothing more than to put something on y'all minds,

Sublime lines of a thought-provoking nature,

Just to make you aware that we've peeped y'all hand,

In a land of democracy, the hypocrisy is so evident

Although concealed behind a congealed wall

of legal bureaucracy,

Something has to be done
about the oxymoronic injustices
of our justice system,
And again, I'll ask you,
When will it end?....

Happy Graduation

You have completed a goal,
Which you've set for yourself,
Increased your knowledge of different subjects,
And increased your human wealth,
In a place of confinement,
You've expanded your mind,
Corrected your vision in areas,
In which you were once blinded,
A positive example, you have set for your peers,
Making the most out of your time,
No matter the number of years,
You have made your family proud,
By improving yourself,
You even put your pride to the side,
And humbled yourself,
By accomplishing this positive goal,
You have laid a solid foundation,
And, on the behalf of the tutors and staff,
I want to wish you all a Happy Graduation....

We've Come a Long Way

As I look at old television footage
of the Civil Rights Movement,
I am saddened,
appalled, and angered by the ignorance
and insensitivity of the blatant racism,
Freedom Fighters used as sacrificial lambs,
Given to the demonic wolves of hatred and bigotry,
Peace and police officers negligent in their duties,
Sitting back watching, and at times participating in
unacceptable atrocities,
But, the movement persisted, ensured and survived,
And now looking back on that time,
I am so very thankful to its organizers and contributors,
I am beneficiary of extraordinary measures of sacrifice,
As a people, we have come a long way,
I'm proud to say,
From sharecroppin' to hip hoppin',
The metamorphic transformation of this nation,
Is astounding to me at times,
And disappointing to me at others,
Because, we still have so far to go,
I pray that we continue to grow,
As a people, not just as a race, but as a nation,
Exceeding all realms of our own earthly expectations
But still, we've come a long way....

Journey of My Smile

I'm lost in my thoughts,

Confused by my consequences,

Frustrated with the facility,

Irritated with these incarcerated individuals,

Unaware of my rigid facial expressions,

My once brightly illuminated aura has been dimmed,

Snuffed out by the ominous presence

of failure and disappointment,

My ambition replaced by indolence,

Once striving in the free world society,

Now surviving in the bowels of the judicial system,

My spirit has been crushed

under the weight of my own expectations,

Being a man of faith; I pray,

I wait and I pray,

Adjusting to the situation

Encouraging others in my environment

Fellowshipping with my fellowman,

Blossoming where I've been planted,

Optimistic about my opportunities,

Now seeing an amber of light

at the end of a once dark tunnel,

Rehabilitated thru remorse,

Fueled by the guilt of my absence in my children's lives

to become a better parent,

Ignited by time-soured relationships

to become a better spouse and partner,

Garnering gratitude towards genuine friendly,

Acquired appreciation for non-absentee family members

My prayers have been answered,

The journey has been completed,

And, I've once again found my smile….

Not Forgotten
For My Cousin Jimmell

Remnants of your smile still linger on,

A vibrant personality and so talented with your gift of song,

Your absence in our lives in vividly apparent,

As a brother, a cousin, a son and as a parent,

We will celebrate your birth,

And commemorate your transcendence

from this earthly plain,

Remaining pure of intention and heart,

In hopes of seeing you again,

But, we rest assuredly knowing,

That you are in a better place,

No longer in any type of pain,

And in God's presence you are graced,

With blessing you look down upon us,

The still suffering and downtrodden,

And these are just a few poetic words

to simply let you know,

That you may be gone,

but you are certainly not forgotten....

Promises Unfulfilled

Promises unfulfilled,

Dreams shattered into shards of illusion,

The conclusion being frustration,

Ponderment of one's judgement,

Drudging through one-side relationships,

Causing you to fellowship with kindred souls,

Exchanging stories told of situations

that have taken a toll

on one's trust of others,

Smothering out the raging flame of reliance,

because of it's non-compliance

in the lives of men in confinement,

This imprisonment doesn't have to be walls or bars,

but the mental scars

caused by the scrapes and pains of life in general,

A clinical diagnosis of paranoia,

And sometimes rightfully so,

All because of promises unfulfilled.

Anointed Message

I may not have been appointed to this position,
But, there's an anointing on my calling,
My formal education
for this situation is my personal experiences,
I may not have studied abroad,
But, if you walk a mile in my shoes;
you might just turn around to take the road less traveled.
You might even marvel at my mastery
of the idiosyncrasies of mankind,
While some of these so-called visionaries are blind
to the basic fundamentals of the human mind,
Man, by nature, is a provider and protector,
By any means necessary for his family,
He will provide food and shelter,
Now some of these methods may not be lawful,
which is awful,
But, is it worse than letting your family starve and freeze,
Suffering from a death far worse than some disease,
With the economical rollercoaster of our society,
Most Americans, no matter their level of education,
Are only one or two paychecks away from homelessness,
Job security is simply defenseless against the sporadic-ness
of the workforce,
Forcing a man to make irrational decisions
to justify his actions in sustaining his family's well-being,
Options are limited because of some of his bad decisions,
And not to mention,
some of the single-parent households being ran by women,
Pressurized and polarized to summarize their situation,
Used to being along for so long,
When they finally do get a man,
They jostle for position in the household hierarchy,
While the children are the ones who suffer,

Diluting the potency of the family structure,
Young men are not sure who to model themselves after:
their father or mother,
Young women don't value the presence
of a father-figure in the household,
Probably because of their mother's emotions towards men
have turned them so cold,
Or maybe because of the lack of respect men show towards
women is so bold,
Whatever the reason for this conduct,
It's up to us to construct a more solid family foundation
Starting with "us"-- the fathers,
The patriarch of the family,
From inauguration to its culmination, I am but one man,
And this is just my observation after careful examination
I must remind you that I haven't been appointed,
but anointed,
And my formal education is my personal experience….

Scandal of Your Love

I use to want to be your Harrison,

Because, I would and wanted to be your personal gladiator,

Protecting you from any harm that would come your way,

And at the end of the day,

I wanted us to have that magnetic love attraction

like Olivia and Fritz.

I wanted to give your clit love fits,

As I licked and strummed your love instrument,

I wanted us to escape this local place and rendezvous,

on an island like Olivia and Jake,

And I'll be at your command,

All of your hopes, dreams, and fears,

I would try to understand,

I go crazy like Huck,

Just thinking about another man touching you,

I'm protective, yet unpredictable,

Deranged, yet contained by your tongue,

Your style and sex appeal are incomparable,

You're my Olivia,

And that's why I'm caught up in,

The scandal of your love....

A Love Poem

Floating,

Elevated by the elation of love,

Drifting,

Aimlessly and shamelessly,

Into the essence of an emotion,

Remorseless,

Liberated by the release,

of my sense of sensibility,

Hopefully,

Yet, still intrigued by its uncertainty,

Reinvigorated,

Relishing in the totality of each passing moment,

Joyful,

Happy to be able to enjoy,

The summits and plummets of love….

Child Abuse

There's a thin line between discipline and child abuse,

And when that transparent line is crossed

Respect and trust from the child you will often lose,

Displays of discipline shouldn't always be violent,

A forecast of corporal punishment

doesn't always have to be the climate,

I am a firm believer in chastising a child

as a method of correcting behavior issues,

But bully-parenting is a perfect example of authority misuse,

Talk to your child first,

Explaining the error of their ways,

Get to the root of the problem of why they misbehave,

Discuss their problems to see why they are acting out,

An although they may show displeasure and pout,

This method is very effective, if you just open your mouth,

As well as your hearts and ears,

Be there to wipe away and not be the cause of their tears,

Being a parent or guardian is a temperamental situation,

And teaching the youth right from wrong

is just one of our obligations,

Whooping and spankings should be the last resort,

Showing vivid and clear love,

That welts and bruises can distort,

Keep in mind that there's a thin line
between discipline and child abuse,
And when that transparent line is crossed,
Respect and trust from the child you will often lose....

Holiday Blues

Holidays are meant to commemorate
a historical or religious event,
But, when you're away from your love ones
and that time of celebration with them isn't spent,
It's hard.
Isolation on these days can leave one emotionally curbed,
perturbed, and disturbed,
And, if you've never been in my situation,
You might find my statements absurd.
Holidays can remind you
that a loved one is no longer around,
Causing suppressed feelings of pain to rain down,
Suicide statistics are elevated for this reason.
Lost loves and loneliness are amplified
during the holiday season,
So, I urge all who have a choice,
In the company that you choose,
Spend time with your family and real friends,
And avoid having the "Holiday Blues"....

Being In-Love

Call me a hopeless romantic,
Or, maybe I'm just in love with the thought of being in love,
You see, I haven't felt that love compulsion in sometime,
Pulsating though my veins,
And oh, how I long to feel the euphoria again,
The not wanting to leave her presence,
And when I do leave,
I return bearing presents, just to let her know
that she's been the cause of my spontaneous effervescence
Trying to anticipate her thoughts, wants and needs,
And, me totally devoid of greed,
As I selflessly share any and everything,
with that special someone.
I want to be the water that quenches
a chosen woman's thirst,
I want to be the nourishment
that sustains and satisfies her vitality,
We'll be exclusively complicit and explicit with one another,
Maybe I'm just dreaming of wishful thinking,
Hoping that my fantasy,
one day, materializes into my reality,
But until then,
I'll patiently wait until I fall in love again….

The Way I Play the Game

So, now you want to be a referee,
And, control the way I play the game,
You see the rules of engagement
were established when the whistle blew,
That means that you can't change or rearrange
the guidelines just to suit you,
I didn't mean to be offensive
because of the way I play the field,
Or, put you on the defensive
simply because of the way I make you feel,
I don't mean to be cold,
by reminding you that I'm a free agent,
Personal stats and individual accomplishments
are what makes me smile,
And, although it may seem like we're playing
for the same team,
We might have very different goals in mind,
Yours might be long term,
With ambitious of retiring from your team,
Something like a marriage,
Where mines might be short term,
A journeyman,
Bouncing from team to team,
Season to season,
Selfishly self-serving my own personal reason,

But, don't worry, cause when I'm in the game,
I give it my all,
You admire the way I hit that hole at full speed,
And that's probably why you want me to sign
a long-term deal,
So, I'm asking you to please try to refrain,
Maintain my spirit, quit trying to contain,
And just simply enjoy the way I play the game....

Do Black Lives Matter?

Do black lives matter?
Trayvon Martin was killed for walking while black
And wearing a hoodie,
Armed with a pack of Skittles,
His killer was tried in court and set free,
Do black lives matter?
Michael Brown was killed
because the officer found him imposing,
The dash cam footage was conveniently absent,
His crime---------- petty theft of some cigars,
The grand jury decided
that there was not enough evidence to indict,
His killer was set free,
Do black lives matter?
Eric Garner was killed for selling loose cigarettes
in New York City,
Instead of being issued a citation,
He was choked to death by five police officers on film,
Once again, the grand jury said there wasn't enough evidence
to indict any of the officers involved,
His killers were set free,
Do black lives matter?
It doesn't appear that they do to me,

Our brothers are guilty until proven innocent
with their court cases being held in the street,
Officers playing judge, jury, and executioners,
with total exoneration,
And again, I'll ask you,
Do black lives matter?

A Bengals Poem — Who Dey

Who Dey, Who Dey, Who Dey!
I bleed orange and black!
To my team, I'm emotionally attached,
Like a family member,
From September thru December,
My Sundays are like holidays,
Anticipated and celebrated,
Who Dey, Who Dey, Who Dey!
I've been with my team since the 80-81 season,
When we suffered our first Superbowl loss,
Back when we had Kenny Anderson,
Isaac Curtis, and our tight end was named Dan Ross,
I've continued to cheer for my team,
After our 2nd Superbowl defeat,
When we had Boomer, Ickey Woods,
and our DB's were known as the "Swat Team."
Who Dey, Who Dey, Who Dey!
I still cheered for my team,
When we had David Klinger,
Akili Smith, and Ki-Jana Carter
I may have cried tangerine tears,
But it made me cheer that much harder,

From Jeff Blake and Carl Pickens,
To Carson Palmer and Ocho Cinco,
We showed signs of greatness,
But, we still had a way to go,
With TJ, Andy Dalton, and A.J. Green,
I'm was excited about the future of my Bengals team,
But now, with Higgins, Boyd and Chase, And with cool ass Joe Burrow to lead the way,
All I can say is,
Who Dey, Who Dey, Who Dey!

Engage the World

You can be engaged in the world at any age,
Just image yourself as the star and the world as your stage,
Take your craft seriously,
in whatever profession that you choose,
Always put your best foot forward,
To ensure respect for yourself and from others
you will not lose,
Diligently chase your passions,
Eluding and averting any obstructions in your path,
Believe, wholeheartedly, in yourself,
And, in your faith, please remain steadfast,
No matter where you are in your life,
Always embrace the opportunity to embark on a new chapter,
Savoring each moment that you breathe,
Creating memories full of love and laughter,
Working hard towards your goals is very important,
to say the least,
Keep your priorities in order
and that includes your family,
Always keep God first,
Because, that's where your strength lies,
And moved diligently along your path, and be sure to set
your aspirations high,
Remember, the only thing worse
than a failure is a person that doesn't even try....

New Year Resolutions

Most people commemorate the start of a new year
with a New Year Resolution,
Initially reinvigorated by a fresh start,
As if it's the answer to solve their problems,
An instant solution to what is, most often,
a long-term problem,
A microcosm of the state of our society,
Everyone seeking immediate gratification and instant results,
Setting themselves up for failure and disappointment,
You see, zest and zeal aren't attributes that you can turn off
and on like a light switch,
So, ditch the notion of doing so,
Drive, determination, and self-motivation
are qualities of a trained behavior,
Although, some people have them as an inherit part
of their human nature,
But, for those who don't,
Late night exercise info-mercials,
And the beginning of a new year
culminate in a resolution of dire straits,
I don't mean to rain on anyone's parade,
But, I do want to shed light on the charade
that we play on ourselves,

I want to hit the gym,

But, I haven't did so much as a push-up in years,

I want to quit smoking, but I'm up to a pack-a-day,

I want to save money, but I'm already thousands in debt,

So, instead of making New Year Resolutions

to insta-fix prolonged problems,

Make concrete lifestyle changes

with stair-stepped goals,

Short and long term,

Persistently and consistently intertwine,

And maybe, you'll find this to be the solution

to your New Year Resolution.

2014 in Review

2014 has been a year full of tragedies and triumphs,

Packed with ups and downs,

The San Antonio Spurs won the NBA title,

And the Seattle Seahawks won the Superbowl Crown,

Lebron James left Miami,

He took his talents back home,

Derek Jeter retired,

But let's not forget about who God called home,

Rest in Peace Rudy Dee,

Maya Angelou, Robin Williams, and Big Bank Hank,

From the Sugar Hill Gang,

And lets' give props where props are due,

This year Taylor Swift did her thang,

The Polar Vortex battered the East Coast,

With several feet of snow,

While the West Coast suffered through severe drought,

The Democrats lost the mid-term elections badly,

Losing both the Senate and the House,

Speaking of politics,

Things can't remain the same,

Michael Brown and Eric Garner

shouldn't have had to lose their lives,

Before we start a conversation about change,
It seems this year the world went crazy,
With the fixation on Big Booty Anthems
lead by Nicki Menage, J.Lo, and Iggy,
And Megan Trainor also did her duty,
Yeah, 2014 was a year of scandals,
None more evident than Bill Cosby's reputation,
in the court of public opinion,
Except, maybe, the bank accounts of suspended NFL
Players Ray Rice and Adrian Peterson,
Malaysia Airlines had two tragedies,
While ISIS militants lost their minds,
The Ebola Virus had the West Coast of Africa
searching for a cure,
That American workers somehow managed to find,
In a year, when every child was singing Frozen's theme song
"Let it Go,"
And every adult was trying to make viral videos,
This year made an historical impact,
I pray that our social consciousness continues to grow,
But, 2014 is now a wrap….

Wait for Me

I need you to wait for me,
It's no illusion that I'm still in love with you,
It's as crystal clear as the tears that form in my eyes
when I hear the sound of your voice,
And, if the choice was mine, I'd be caressing and undressing
you at this very moment in time,
But, unfortunately,
the circumstances won't allow it to be,
So, until I return home,
I'm asking you to wait for me,
We were lovers and best friends,
And that doesn't have to end,
I just need you to wait for me,
They didn't lie when they said that,
"Absence makes the heart grow fonder,"
Because, the longer I'm away from you,
The more I realize how you complete me,
And if you allow me back in your life,
I'll be the man that you need me to be,
And the father that your son needs.
You're the wind beneath my wings,
The melody in my song,
The way that you look at me
motivates me to be the best I can be,
I just wanted you to know how I feel about you,
And baby, I just need you to wait for me….

Black History

Black history is a mystery that needs to be discovered by all,
For this new generation to understand the reasons
behind the pain of the freedom call,
Children being torn from their mother's arms,
As our forefathers stood helpless,
Petrified by the threat of severe bodily harm,
Generations subjected to inhumane conditions
and mistreatment,
Our minds being conditioned
to accept the mistreatment,
Inventions and ingenuity being exploited,
Good people being oppressed
by the appointed claiming they're anointed,
A race of people stripped of their religion,
customs, and beliefs,
But, they survived and thrived through it all,
To become the best that they could be,
So let me give you some black history,
If I may enlighten you,
Here are a list of names just to name a few,
Harriet Tubman escaped from slavery
and help set other slaves free,
And we had some great educators,
Like Frederick Douglass, Booker T. and W.E.B.

We had some great inventors,
Like Elijah McCoy, Richard Spikes,
and George Washington Carver,
They helped improve the lives of man,
And helped us grow much farther,
Dr. Mae Jemison and Guion Bluford,
Were the first black man and woman to travel to space,
Expanding the minds and horizons of the entire black race,
We had some great leaders,
Like Malcolm X, Medgar Evers, and Dr. Martin Luther King,
They all lost their lives to help us realize their own dreams,
This is just the tip of the iceberg of our black history,
And you can do your own research,
So, it doesn't have to remain a mystery….

I Love What You Bring to the Table

I love what you bring to the table,
Besides your beauty and intellect,
Your confidence, ladylike swagger
and attitude of "No-regrets,"
Plus, your incomparable compassion
for those that you love,
It's more than attractive,
It's symbolically pure,
Like the wings of a flying white dove,
I love what you bring to the table,
A powerful, yet sexy presence,
a gansta-ish, but still regal essence,
The way you carry yourself,
Commanding the room's attention,
Boss chick status,
I ain't even gonna mention,
Cool, calm, and relaxed,
From you I'm never sensing and tension,
Unless a muthafucka take you there,
I love what you bring to the table,
Don't let some chick step out of line,
You're quick to check their ass,
Make a weak bitch almost cry,
And don't let some dude get out of pocket,
You'll tighten his ass up,

Quick, fast, and in a hurry like a wrench to a socket,

I love what you bring to the table,

Your full, sexy lips and curvaceous thighs,

Your beautiful chocolate skin and your seductive eyes,

Damn! Just thinking about you

does something to me,

Something far beyond my comprehension,

You got my manhood standing up at full attention,

And baby I love what you bring to the table….

I Wanna Thank You God

I wanna thank you God,
Thank you for all you have done and continue to do for me,
I wanna thank you for my health, my safety, and my sanity,
I just wanna give you the praise that you so rightfully deserve,
I wanna thank you for never forsaking me and always keeping your word,
I just wanna thank you God,
I wanna thank you for making a way when I couldn't see it,
I wanna thank you for rescuing me every time I need it,
I wanna thank you for the gifts and talents you've bestowed upon me,
And for allowing me to believe in myself,
I wanna thank you for intervening at times I didn't realize I needed your help,
I just wanna thank you Heavenly Father,
I wanna thank you for my children and for always watching over them,
I wanna thank you for always guiding and protecting them,
I wanna thank you for my family and real friends,
I wanna thank you for the ones, in which I can truly depend,
I just wanna thank you father,
I wanna thank you for all that you do,
I wanna thank you for sustaining me,
And for turning my twos into fews,

I wanna thank you Heavenly Father,

I just wanna thank you for blessing me,

I wanna thank you for your patience in molding me,

I wanna thank you for loving me,

Even at times when I didn't love myself,

I just wanna thank you for being you,

Above all else,

And for that reason alone,

I wanna thank you,

Thank you, Heavenly Father….

I Wanna Go Home

I wanna go home,

Home is where I feel safe,

Where I feel loved and wanted,

Home is where I feel needed and appreciated,

Where I can let my guard down and relax,

I wanna go home,

Home is where I am happy,

Where I can smile and laugh,

There's no judgment at home,

Only acceptance from my family,

Home embraces me with open arms,

I wanna go home,

Home shelters and comforts me,

Home doesn't place blame and isn't ashamed of me,

Where I feel protected and never neglected,

Home is where I feel affection and admiration,

I'm missing that right now,

And I just wanna go Home….

Respected Man

A respected man blurs the line
between being in control and compassion,
Understands that in order to be respected,
you have to give respect,
A liaison between the common-man and the "establishment."
The buffer between the voice-less and the institution,
A respected man, who has earned the admiration of the
hierarchy, his co-workers, and the men that he is in charge of,
Soft-spoken, yet commanding the room's attention,
I'm speaking about a respected man, if I've failed to mention,
Your presence, once you are gone, will be surely missed
by all you have encountered,
But, we understand that it's time for you to move on,
And, we sincerely wish you the best,
I want you to know, beyond a shadow of a doubt,
You're a man who has earned everybody's respect….

Who Are You

Who are you?
Who are you when the observing eye is obscured,
And the blustery crowds have subsided,
When you're in a place where silence surrounds,
A place where serenity and tranquility
astounds,
Who are you?
Who are you when nobody is watching,
When you are standing on the crutches
of solitude & seclusion,
When you are put in a position where your morality
can be called into question,
Who are you?
Who are you when the choices are prosperity or integrity,
When the options are doing what's legal
or doing what's right,
Would your honesty surprise or would selfishness prevail,
I surmise that the struggle would cause you travail,
The question is simple,
When the only eyes that are watching you,
are the ever-seeing eyes of God,
Who are you?

Imagine if Women Were Cars

I don't mean to be mean or demean anyone with this piece,
My strategy is to, simply, use this analogy
as my form of poetic release,
But, gentleman just imagine our relationships with the
women in our lives like the relationships
we have with our cars,
Where some are to be pampered and stored carefully;
while others are neglected and dogged out so hard,
Side-pieces and jump-offs are just like "sliders"
never claimed by anyone,
But, every Tom, Dick, and Harry can jump inside her,
Rental cars are the equivalent to prostitutes and whores,
Sometimes necessary and always temporary,
And their quality depends on the price you paid for her,
Baby mamas are different and often hard to describe,
Like that one car you've got so much invested in that you
can't even get rid of that ride,
Most girlfriends and long-term relationships are like bargains
or the whip in which you feel you got a deal,
A solid investment getting you from point A to point B and
occasionally providing a home-cooked meal,
But, just like most used cars
when their miles get high and their value drops,
You leave them parked in the driveway or trade them in for
somebody else to cop,

Wives are like dream cars; special to you in every way,
Big Ticket items that you hope to one day afford
and have in your possession someday,
And, if you are fortunate to have that lady/luxury vehicle in your life,
Be sure you service her with attention, love, and affection,
and always treat her right,
Once again, my purpose for this piece was not to devalue or demean,
But, to simply shed light on how we as men treat our ladies/prize possessions among other things….

It's Time to Wake Up

Now, don't get me wrong,
I accept full responsibility for my state of humility,
The point has been well taken,
The problem has been solved,
But, they still want to keep me incarcerated,
I think they're trying to break my resolve,
It seems like they're trying to dissolve my hopes & dreams,
No judicial, halfway house, or early release,
Oh, I get it now,
Prisons are big business,
The inmates are the hot commodity,
But, the system is the one who will ultimately capitalize
off of our demise,
I thought the justice system was supposed to be about justice
and not just profits,
But, I'm sadly mistaken,
Visibly shaken from my findings,
My eyes have been pried open,
To a revelation to which I was once blind,
But, the veil has been removed,
My mood has been moved,
From victim to advocate,
And, I'm not having it any longer,

The more people we inform,

The stronger we get as a people,

And now, they have reason to sound the alarm,

Especially now, that we know the designed assignment of the justice system,

It's a systemic slavery for "Just-Us"

And my brothas & sistahs, it's time for us to wake up!

Public Service Announcement

I used to go by "Ron C,"

When I was rappin',

Big time drug dealin', hustlin', and trappin',

Glorifying foolishness in my lyrics,

Funding my own pipedreams,

So that anybody could hear it,

But, that me is a person of the past,

100 lbs. packs thru UPS,

I knew it was too good to last,

I broke the rules,

I did the crime,

Years behind bars,

I did the time,

Kept my mouth shut,

Never pointed fingers at other dudes,

I'm the last of a dying breed,

These fools playin' by different rules,

Flat-out tellin' like that shit's cool,

In the game now, I'm a dinosaur amongst space-ships,

I'm a rollin' factory,

While these young cats got 30-inch rims on they whips,

The game changes before you know it,

Switched my name to "Brotha Poet,"

Trying to catch the attention of those young men
who are willing to listen,
I want to re-route them from taking the same path
that I once took,
Prompt them to use their gift of foresight,
before they get a first-hand look,
From behind bars,
Criminally profiled for driving a flashy car,
Rockin' $100 dollar t-shirts and $500 dollar jeans,
Pulverized priorities trying to impress ghetto queens,
Most of them will leave you hanging in the dust,
Trust me,
I've been in those shoes,
Been in that same situation,
I've paid them dues,
Take heed to this warning,
So you won't have to go thru what I've been thru,
Finish high school,
Go to college,
Pay attention in class,
Acquire some knowledge,
Get a career and a family of your own,
Get a (401 K) and purchase you a home,
Be a productive citizen in all that you do,
Take it from me, "Brotha Poet,"
Cause, if you choose the wrong route,
They have a prison cell waiting just for you….

Find Out Who You Are

People always say things like,
"Be the best that you can be!"
Or "Live up to your full-potential,"
But, it's hard to be your best,
When you don't exactly know what you want to be,
Life is like a rollercoaster ride,
You get on where you're born,
Then, during your formative years of infancy,
childhood, and adolescence,
The ride inches forward and upward
towards the precipice of adulthood,
And then, suddenly, the gravity of life takes over,
Taking you on a series of twists, turns, and loops
associated with being a grown up,
And, if you haven't been properly prepared for life, or in
other words,
If you haven't braced yourself for the ride,
The journey can and will be more than likely overwhelming,
Leaving you frazzled, disoriented, and often
discombobulated about the choices you have made,
So, in order to make an informed decision about this
rollercoaster ride that we call life,
Do the required research that will help you come
to a concrete conclusion and direction,

And, in the future,

when the tracks of existence become unstable,

The safety precautions of preparation won't allow you to fail or derail,

Ensuring you and your family a solid foundation,

So, enjoy the ride and pave the way for your future generations....

Prison Greeting Card

I know that this time apart hasn't been easy on you,
In my heart, it's like you're doing this time with me,
Baby, I want you to know,
It's because of the fond memories that we've shard together
that make these lonely days and nights somewhat bearable,
I apologize if I don't express how I love and appreciate
having you in my life as often as I know I should,
No amount of time or distance could change
how I feel about you and yours,
I know that things haven't been going as smooth for us
as we both would like,
And, I'm sorry for my part in that,
I need you to know that in this marathon of life
that we are living,
I want to go the distance with you,
You complete me,
You make me want to be a better man,
I just need for you to be patient with me,
I'm asking for you to continue to wait for me,
Simply, because the love and bond that we share are worth it,
I love and I miss you more than mere words
can truly express,
And baby, I hope you can forgive me….

Desire

No matter what you do,
If you plan to succeed,
You have to want to be the best,
So, lace them shoes up tight
Get ready for the fight,
Because your desire will surely be put to the test,
Whatever the craft,
You'll need a strong work ethic,
Steadily build up your skill set,
Like you're doing calisthenics,
Your drive has to be fast and furious,
You have to be passionate, tenacious, and voracious,
Because sometimes you might be scrutinized and ostracized
for your convictions and beliefs,
So, stand as firm as the concrete beneath your feet,
For what you believe,
Put your best foot forward,
So that you can achieve,
The desire of your heart in which you've dreamed,
Because, no matter what you do,
If you plan to succeed,
You have to want to be the best,
So, lace your shoes up tight,
And get ready for a fight,
Because your desire will surely be put to the test…

Another Prayer

Lord, I'm tired of getting locked up

Please, help me make a change,

I keep making bad decisions

There's gotta be a better way!

I'm tired of wasting days

And having sleepless nights,

The devil keeps on testing me,

I gotta put up a fight!

I know right from wrong,

But, doing wrong feels so right,

6 yrs behind bars.

I don't wanna waste my life,

Missed my kids' graduations,

And I ain't even found a wife,

I'm repentin' for my sins,

I'm so tired of living trife,

If I gotta struggle,

Then it is what it is,

Cut hair and sell books,

I'll start another biz,

Live life with a purpose!

I'm doing my family a dis-service,

If I don't stand and be a man,

And show em' that they're worth it….

Prison Greeting Card Pt.2

Your laughter reminds me

of what it feels like to be happy,

Your responses to my questions

puts my mind at ease,

You give me reason to believe,

To believe that we will make it thru this mess,

Simply because, it's just a test,

A test of our love for one another and our strong will,

And, where there's a will,

There will always be a way,

And so, I want to thank you,

I thank you for remaining in my life,

Through all the pain, heartache, and strife,

Our reward awaits us on the other side of this storm,

The pot of gold at the end of a long rainbow,

And the ultimate prize being our love and happy life with each other....

If I Came with Instructions

If I came with instructions, you still couldn't handle to me...
In your haste, to explore the nuances of my structure,
You would simply overlook some of the simplicity
of my function,
Turning me on should be second nature.
But yet, you fumble around,
But, if you start at the top, which is my mind,
You would know that's where the primary buttons are found.
Fascinated by my outer appeal,
Impressed by the first impression of upgrade,
You think you know how to handle me,
Because, my form is similar to something you delt wit
before,
So, before you encase me in the Otter box of life,
which is marriage,
Take the time to learn that I am so much more,
Once my novelty wears off and I'm no longer a trophy
or an object admiration,
Will I be tossed in a drawer and cast to the side like past
trinkets that once caught your eye?
Or, will you keep me close to you
like a clip on your hip to be at your disposal?
Will you wake up grabbing for me?...
Will you feel lost without me?...

Will I know every moment of your schedule,

even the times that you forget?

Will I be able to turn you on with a push of a button

and leave you soaking wet?

I see you out here searching around and checking for

something like me,

So, be careful what you ask for, because once you get it

even with instructions, you still couldn't handle me...

Give Me My Flowers Now

Give me my flowers now!
Don't wait till I'm dead and gone,
Unless you're being fake and phony about it
and really happy to see me move on,
Give me my flowers now
if you want to put a smile on my face,
Unless you showing up at my funeral
was simply for you to save face,
Give me my flowers now!
So, while I'm alive we can enjoy each other's time,
Unless your reasons for bringing flowers to my funeral
was to see my grieving wife cry,
Give me my flowers now!
Unless you feel guilty about something you did wrong,
You might be the first one to shed a tear when they start to
sing sad songs,
Bring me my flowers now!
So, we can discuss your current situations,
Instead of waiting for me to pass
to become the topic of your conversation,
Bring my flowers now!
So, I can enjoy them while I'm alive,
Cause, bringing me flowers when I'm dead and gone,
to me, it just doesn't seem right.
Love on your people while they're here, leave no mystery,
make sure that the love is shown loud and clear.

Aging Love

Beggers borrow,

Lovers quarrel,

And God's love is Still the same,

Hissy fits from scorned lovers lips,

And time can only lessen the pain,

Once passionate flames burned,

Life's vivid pages have been turned,

And now, ashy ambers lay a smolder,

Gravity pulled aging signs,

Pierce your hearts vanity

 Like prickly needles pines,

Of a purposeful life that's growing older.....

Who Got Next?

Whose got next?
And, I'm not talking about a game,
I'm asking who has next?
Because, the leadership of today has me feeling ashamed,
Baby boomers are retiring
and 30–50-year-olds are in control,
And, I'm not really sure that's a good thing,
because he who has next is going to follow our mold,
I hope whoever has next is more concerned about their future
than the current situation of today,
Unlike our city government, who's already spent their
retirement away,
From brown outs to street cars,
The wasteful spending has gone too far,
And now, they want to privatize parking meters
and parking lots,
Using the profits from overpriced license plate sales
to build brand new jails and gambling spots,
I hope the youth of today is paying attention,
Because, some of the things I shouldn't have to mention,
we're being force-fed these issues on the daily From 5, 9, 12,
and Fox,

But, with the infusion of new blood in our government,
Some of these issues will stop,
Blur the lines with bipartisanship,
And, the way they're treating Obama
should never be overlooked,
But simply, take it for what it is, a group of greedy people
showing their hand,
Vetoes and government shutdowns
just to spite this one black man
I'm hopeful for today,
But, optimistic for tomorrow's threats,
Can't wait for today's youth to grow up
And say hey .... We got next!

A Glorious Story

I should feel rage,

Because of all the years, I spent caged up like an animal,

But, I don't,

I should be shedding tears

for putting myself in a position

to be isolated and separated from my family,

But, I won't,

I can't question the plan that God has scripted,

For this one black man that some may consider as gifted,

Is that an accurate illustration or depiction?

The answer is "yes",

Because, my reality is so non-fiction,

A glorious story of rags to riches,

Perfectly written so well,

That it sounds made up like fiction,

Years stored away,

Warehoused on a shelf like the potter's clay,

But, God's word was the water that rehydrated the cracks and crevices of my soul,

That had been slowly drying out,

From the wretched effects of a world that's so cold,

I should feel hurt and pain,

Because of the years of mental and emotional strain,

I've put on my four children,

But instead, I feel numb,

I'm astoundingly proud of the responsible

young man and women that they have become,

They continued to thrive during my absence,

Not letting my mayhem cave or collapse their building,

blocks of success,

So, how could I be mad,

At my God,

My Savior,

My Dad,

I can't,

I won't.

I am not,

In fact,

I'm so thankful for all the blessings that I've got,

So, I don't question the plan that God had scripted

For this one black man that some may consider as gifted,

It's more than an accurate illustration or depiction,

In fact, it's my reality so non-fiction,

A glorious story of rags to riches,

Written so perfectly well that it sounds made up like fiction…

I Cry for My People

I cry for my people,

I cry for the former Kings and Queens

of a strong black nation,

Who were tricked,

Kidnapped,

And made to work on southern plantations,

I cry for my people,

I cry for the male slaves that were beaten and abused,

I cry for the female slaves who were raped and misused,

I cry for the children who were never educated and left destitute,

I cry for my people,

I cry for lives lost in this land in which we live,

I cry for the many sacrifices for freedom

that we have still yet to give,

I cry for my people,

I cry for the victims of the rampant police brutality,

I cry for the families and protestors

who could easily become a causality,

I cry for this nation,

I cry for this country,

I cry for my people…

The Land of the Free

The land of the free,

The home of the brave,

The home of the slave trade that made kings turn to slaves,

The land where it's supposed to be "justice" for us all,

But, that included everybody, but "just-us" y'all,

The land that's left a bitter taste in our mouth,

Like the taste of "whites-only" pie,

The bitter taste of the tears we've cried,

As we have watched our people die,

Gun downed like hogs lead to the slaughter,

Mothers and Fathers beaten and chased by dogs

As they tried to fight for rights of their sons and daughters,

A far cry from the Constitution we interpret,

Rhetoric that's insidiously intrepid,

Leaving my people destitute and decrepit,

Where our dreams look like mirages,

Beaten back to reality while we duck and dodge

the Billy-clubs they slug us with,

They get so high off an adrenaline rush from the chase

that they mistake a gun for the taser on their hip,

Now ain't that a trip,

But the only trip we will be taking is to the morgue,

And to the funeral home

where our families will mourn our loss,

And the example-less children

raised without a parent

are the ones who will ultimately pay the cost,

In the land of the free,

The home of the brave,

The home of the slave trade that made kings turn to slaves….

Vocal Defecation

Excuse me for spewing this verbal urination,

or for dumping this vocal defecation,

because some may say that I'm just talkin' shit,

Well maybe just a lil bit,

Because in every lie there's a hint of the truth,

Just like in most fruit

there's a seed that can produce more fruit,

You feel me…

Well, maybe not… if I'm not in arm's reach,

But I know you can hear me,

So, listen up while I preach,

And if by chance you learn something,

I won't even mind if you call me teach,

See, I've been blessed with the gift of vocab,

Honed my craft while I was away at social rehab,

Came back glowing from my abduction

like I had been probed on a space craft,

Now you do the math,

Cause this shit don't add up,

You see, I was just one of many,

Who chose to get my mind right,

When it should have been plenty,

Long days and longer nights,

But they was lost in a sauce, that wasn't as thick as Ragu,

They chose to stay with the old,

Guess they wasn't ready to embrace the new,

But, if they knew what I know about life,

Looking back in hindsight,

They would've chose differently,

Maybe chose to get their screws tight,

Because, during my journey of life,

I've been many things,

I've seen many things,

I've seen so many fake faces,

I've seen so many girls make nasty-ass fuck faces,

I'm sorry maybe that was tasteless,

But, sometimes you don't get to choose the car in which you ride or with whom you drive,

Sometimes you just go along for the ride and watch the dove's cry,

Big crocodile tears that can blur your vision,

Muthafuckas sitting around moping about their bad decisions,

Shittt! But not me,

I was born a winner,

I sleep with passion,

And eat success for dinner,

Fuck Facebook Instagram and Tender

I like that personal touch,

I still like writing on a paper page,

And I love this microphone I clutch when I touch the stage

So, you must excuse me for spewing this verbal urination,

or for dumping this vocal defecation,

because some may say that I'm just talkin' shit,

Well maybe just a lil bit,

Because, in every lie, there's a hint of the truth,

Just like in most fruit,

there's a seed that can produce more fruit,

Now ain't that the truth,

You feel me….

Welcome to the Jungle

Welcome to the jungle
Where only the strong survive,
Where you best get yo weight up,
If you plan to stay alive,
They call this the slammer, the Big House, and the Pen,
Where yo days and nights last forever,
Seem like they ain't gone never end,
Well, it's time to man yo ass up,
All that whining and crying gotta stop,
You done got yo self locked up with the wolves,
And, they can't wait to take yo young ass up top,
They don't care if you are a first-time offender
You gone find out how real shit can get,
No fake actors, no paid pretenders,
Just the harsh concrete and steel reality,
Where you have to constantly watch your back,
Unless you wanna end up a casualty,
And since you want to travel down the wrong road,
Get ready to listen to all the sob and war stories,
That are constantly being told,
And speaking of being told,
The guards tell you everything to do,
When to eat, go to sleep, and even when to use the bathroom,
Yeah, it sounds crazy don't it?
But, it's real talk, no jive
So, welcome to the jungle,
Where only the strong will survive....

The Revolution Will be Televised

Whoever said that the revolution would not be televised,

could not have foreseen the world that we live in today,

It's no longer a society of closed caption,

But, a generation of social media,

Where everything is an open attraction,

Causing desensitivity and distractions like a bully

picking on the mentally challenged,

When, he in fact has issues of his own,

Minute topics are always overblown,

Simply because of the frequency of the tweets

that are shown,

Who really care if the dress was black and blue

or white and gold,

The real issues are being camouflaged

by a barrage of bullshit,

But, the revolution will be televised,

It's just sad that only a few will be able to see it,

Only the truly conscious

will be able to decipher the authentic,

From the smoke screen of the fraudulent,

Sort of like the white woman,

who was president of the NAACP in her city,

Her hard work shamed and defamed,

because of her race,

Now that's the real pity,

And ironically, now she truly knows
what it means to be black,
The revolution has already started,
and our brothas and sistahs are being killed on the frontline,
Please believe,
Nowhere is safe,
From a simple traffic stop to Bible study prayer groups,
Please pray for the eight souls who lost their lives,
From New York to Baltimore,
From Ferguson to South Carolina,
There's a nationwide epidemic of racial injustice,
And the hashtags are wasted on the mundane,
Callused minds are being trained by violent video games,
What a negligent crying shame,
A clear sign of the times,
In this day and age,
But, the revolution will be televised,
And the social media world will be the stage,
It's just sad that everybody won't be able to see it….

Depression

I'm trying to shake this feeling,
I'm trying to shake it like the red, gold, and brown
Leaves that fall from the trees in the fall-time season,
But, I can't for some odd reason,
The dark clouds of gloom hover over me in a fog of pity,
Blinding me from seeing any glimpse of happiness,
Sadness and despair are intertwined in my mindset,
Woven deeply into the fabric of my very existence,
But, I must persist and continue this fight
on the battlefield of my mind,
The war has been waged in silence,
But, I refuse to be a slave to this chemical imbalance that
leaves me feeling this way,
Many will not understand my struggle,
Some may say that I'm weak-minded and simply can't cope
with the hands of cards that life has dealt me,
But, that's not the case at all,
On the outside looking in, everything appears to be fine,
As I smile to hide the pain that I struggle with from within,
I'm trying to regain the happiness that I once knew,
I'm fighting for normalcy in my life once again,
I'm battling the wretched enemy known as depression....

You'll Understand Once You Get Older

My mama always said, that when I got older I'd understand,
And, now that I've gotten to be a certain age,
I can now clearly see what she was talking about,
The gap in the generations is as evident
as the crack in the famous Liberty Bell,
An even more irreparable by comparable standards,
You see, I'm from a generation where children
were seen and not heard,
Now-a-days, kids are quick to voice their opinions
 Some verbally embarrass their parents
and even try to get the last word.
I would've gotten smacked senseless,
But, today's parents are defenseless against their onslaught,
They are fearful of getting arrested
or maybe even a worse outcome like getting they ass shot,
Today's kids are exposed to way too much,
And with the touch of a fingertip, they can see things
that would be disgusting and revolting to the average adult,
But, they don't flinch not even an inch,
Simply because, they're already seen much worse,
On Twitter, Instagram, or a Facebook post,
While social media can be some of the most unsociable
and impersonal behavior that you can engage in,
Kids hiding behind comfortable facades,

They'd rather text than talk,

They "sext" and wonder why they get stalked

They are hashtag bullies,

Twitter re-tweet gangstas.

The only real beef they've had came with

Mash potatoes and gravy at a Sunday dinner,

But you still can't tell em' shit,

Technology is now their teacher,

However, they will ultimately become students of life itself,

Learning from heartache, pain, and strife throughout

A lifetime of experiences that will scold them

And mold them simultaneously,

And just like my mama told me,

They will understand when they get older….

Beauty is More Than Skin Deep

I've been entangled in a web,
Entrapped by a barrage of mirages
of diamond encrusted fantasies.
It's been entrenched in my mind
That's why it's hard for me
to find a different way to think,
Staring at girls whose eyelashes
have their own sets of eyelashes when they blink.
If the woman that I choose is a reflection of me,
What assets am I choosing to view
when I lay my eyes on thee?
Is it your outer appearance that can be altered
with one trip to the hair store?
Or, is it your inner beauty that has left a lasting impression
& leaves me wanting more...
You see, with the invention of hair extensions
and girls wearing more paint on their faces
than all the canvases in every art exhibit across the nation,
It's hard for me to realize who you really are,
until the emotions have got us caught up
& we've gone too far
Let's find the time to rewind,
& go back in time to a place
where you knew a girl liked you for you

& there weren't any preconceived notions,
all she knows is that you were love's potion…
And that you guys were meant to be together
laughing on the phone until one of you fell asleep,
You hang up first, no, you hang up first,
I'm sitting here getting weak at just the thought of that,
How many of us went thru that, experienced that,
enjoyed that, and miss that?
Sometimes maturity leads to misconceptions
or gives you a warped perception of what beauty really is
compared to what you now find attractive
to what you found attractive as a kid-
I think that women should come with labels,
Some would read pretty to the eyesight
but very emotionally unstable
And, I'm sure the ladies will say the same for guys,
Some labels would read, "How he's broke as hell,
but he's easy on the eyes."
So, don't judge a book by its cover,
Cause a pretty woman don't necessarily make her a good
mother. Just like his swag doesn't necessarily make him a
good dad because 9 times outta 10
he never had one to learn from…
So if, we take the time to know one another
before we sleep with each other.
You will find that beauty is more than skin deep.

Be the King You Were Meant To Be

Be the king you were meant to be,

The man your family needs,

and that begins with staying free.

The bible says, "So a man thinketh, so is he."

I claim to be unselfish, but, all I think about is me

I claim to be rehabilitated and say that I know how to act.

But, all the while, I'm thinking I can't wait til I'm released,

so I can go pick up a pack...

You see, I'm not alone in the struggle

with this wrongful mindset...

Vanishing memories of sitting alone in a jail cell,

how quickly we forget...

We talk real slick to our love ones

about how we got it together and ready to make a change...

But, we ain't fooling nobody but ourselves now

Don't that seem strange?...

Most of us feel hopeless and out of luck

because of these felonies that we've obtained...

But all things are possible thru Christ

and if you only use your brain...

You see your head is more than just a hat rack

to fill up with smoke from a $50 kush sack,

Or use to dream up illegal schemes

just to make a few stacks...

All the while saying,

"If it don't make dollars, it don't make sense"...

Well, what sense does it make if those green and gold dreams

Lands you right back into incarceration...

Or maybe even a worse situation

like being maimed for life or even death...

Or do my words fall, on deaf ears?

Yo' spirit looking down on yo' body

sheading crocodile tears..

For a man who never lived up to his full potential...

Saying how you lived for gold chains and fancy cars-

things that we're so non-essential.

Right now my brothers & sisters were at a crossroad.

Where we can break the cycle or let the cycle break us

The choice is truly yours, but in GOD I trust...

There's life in the word,

and death in the temptation of the flesh.

Open up your mind, so you can live life with no regrets...

Now look, I know no one is perfect,

but I'm trying to be a better person.

I'm living my life with a purpose,

simply, because I know my family is worth it.

Be the king you were meant to be...

Be the man you're family needs

and that begins with staying free...

We so often say, I'm not gonna let my family starve.

I'm gonna do what I have to do…

and so often we lose with this jacked up attitude..

forgetting everything we just took our families through.

You see little boys live for image

while grown men imagine how to live.

What sense does it make to have a $2,000 car

with some $5,000 rims?

Like Spike Lee said, "Wake up my brothers up, you wake!"

How much time out of our lives

does the system have to take?

Before you realize

the life you were living was the real lie …

My brother, I beg you to open up your third eye and think.

I mean really think about what you're doing

before your life and your family you ruin …

Be the king you were meant to be…

Be the man your family needs

and that begins with staying free...

Message to Young Black Men

Young, black man be proud of who you are …
you come from a lineage of illumination.
Yeah that's right, you're a real star …
From the shores of Africa to the jail cells of Attica
the enemy wants to oppress you.
Your joy is what he's after…
This Willie Lynch society that we live in
Was designed to hold you down…
Like the welfare system of the 70's
punished black mothers for keeping a father around…
Their plan is simple, cut the head and the body will fall.
They want to eliminate us from our families,
Yes, that's right?. They want it all!!!....
First, they infiltrate our sister's minds,
give them the blueprint to independence,
and turn around and give us time....
Hence fourth, a disconnect begins
A family without a Leader...
Man, what about those kids?
Male seeds left to fend and scrap for chicken feed.
You're taught to kill one another
over simply nothing but greed...

Rock Revivals and Affliction

status quo becomes the addiction,

They are crumbling our foundation

before it's even formed.

Robbing and killing has become the norm...

Desensitized by the monotonous cries

of another grown man asking for help

but, if I put my pride to the side and open my third eye.

And realize helping another black man

is like helping myself.

That light bulb moment...

That moment you realize the bigger picture..

You see it's not about you as an individual,

but about the entirety of the structure,

The black family structure has been broken down

for whatever reasons black fathers

are nowhere to be found.

And the ones that are never get any credit.

We have their own kids thanking Santa Claus

and the Easter Bunny

When daddy really did it

Combat commercialism with realism,

Rebuttal egotism with rationalism...

Think about how you felt as a child

when your father wasn't around…

an instant identity crisis...

No uncles around only mom's boyfriends ...

No one to comfort you when you lost...

Nobody to celebrate with when you finally did win.

Black people, it's time for us to do better...

To rebuild our family structure,

To show our children a positive, healthy household

with a strong, black father and a strong, black mother...

www.ingramcontent.com/pod-product-compliance
Lightning Source LLC
Chambersburg PA
CBHW031630160426
43196CB00006B/350